# Unshackled

# Unshackled

## Breaking Addiction's Chains Through God's Grace

GRAHAM JOSEPH HILL

CASCADE *Books* • Eugene, Oregon

UNSHACKLED
Breaking Addiction's Chains Through God's Grace



Cascade Books
An Imprint of Wipf and Stock Publishers
199 W. 8th Ave., Suite 3
Eugene, OR 97401

www.wipfandstock.com

PAPERBACK ISBN: 979-8-3852-6273-1
HARDCOVER ISBN: 979-8-3852-6274-8
EBOOK ISBN: 979-8-3852-6275-5

*Cataloguing-in-Publication data:*

Names: Hill, Graham Joseph, author.

Title: Unshackled : breaking addiction's chains through God's grace / Graham Joseph Hill.

Description: Eugene, OR : Cascade Books, 2026 | Includes bibliographical references.

Identifiers: ISBN 979-8-3852-6273-1 (paperback) | ISBN 979-8-3852-6274-8 (hardcover) | ISBN 979-8-3852-6275-5 (ebook)

Subjects: LCSH: Habit breaking—Religious aspects—Christianity. | Compulsive behavior—Religious aspects—Christianity. | Church work with recovering addicts.

Classification: BV4598.7 .H55 2026 (paperback) | BV4598.7 (ebook)


VERSION NUMBER 03/17/26

For Gordon Buxton (Bucko): my uncle and soul friend.
You've stood by me through every struggle and joy, carrying burdens, sharing laughter, and living out grace. Your steadfast love and quiet strength have shaped my life more than words can say.
With deepest gratitude, I dedicate these pages to you.

# Contents

# List of Tables

# Prologue

## My Journey to Freedom from Alcohol and Addiction

### Struggling in Secret

WHEN I BEGAN DRINKING in my twenties, I never expected to become addicted to alcohol. In my early years of pastoral ministry, I was passionate, driven, and wanted to serve God and others. But along the way, the pressures of leadership, the emotional toll of caring for others, and my internal battles with anxiety and depression began to wear me down. I felt isolated in my struggles.

Rather than admit my pain or seek help, I turned to alcohol as my escape. Night after night, after long days of ministry, I'd pour myself drinks to numb the stress and sadness I felt inside.

On the outside, I was a successful pastor and theologian (pastoring churches and lecturing at colleges), but on the inside, I was falling apart. I struggled privately with alcoholism and depression even while working as a church pastor. I was terrified that anyone in the church would find out.

This shame drove me to hide my drinking and despair, keeping them locked up and hidden away, afraid that people might find out. Only my wife, family, closest friends, and doctor knew the truth. I felt like a fraud, preaching freedom, hope, and joy to others on Sundays, only to drown my sorrows in secret.

The stigma and guilt were paralyzing. I told myself that a pastor was supposed to have it all together, that admitting my weakness would ruin my ministry. So, I suffered alone, and my addiction worsened over time.

Looking back now, I realize there were early warning signs. I was using alcohol to self-medicate my depression and anxiety. I'd drink until I felt numb, and momentarily, it seemed to ease the relentless ache of sadness.

But the relief was short-lived: the depression only worsened, and I needed more alcohol to keep it at bay.

My situation hit its lowest point when I realized I couldn't get through a day without alcohol. I remember coming home one evening, closing the door to my study with a bottle in hand, and thinking, "This has to stop." After a decade of daily heavy drinking, my life was falling apart. I felt God's heartbreak and my own.

My family life was suffering. Even if I tried to hide it, my wife could see the distance in my eyes, smell the alcohol on my breath, and witness my body falling apart. My young children sensed something was wrong. I wasn't fully present for them. The thought of losing my family's trust or hurting them because of my drinking frightened me. They deserved better from me, and deep down, I knew it.

## Turning Point: Reaching Out for Help

My turning point came in 2005. After years of this downward spiral, I finally reached a breaking point: a moment of clarity and divine intervention. In July 2005, as I reflected on the imminent birth of another daughter, and reflected on whether I wanted to be alive to see her grow up, I decided to stop drinking alcohol altogether.

I vividly remember the day I poured the remaining liquor down the drain and fell to my knees, weeping. I cried out to God for help because I knew I couldn't break free on my own. I'd tried going to an addiction rehabilitation center for help, but hadn't gotten better. I knew I needed God's help to get free, otherwise I'd die from my alcoholism. There was no dramatic vision or instant miracle; instead, there was a resolute conviction in my spirit that I had to choose life or death. I chose life.

I admitted to myself and God that I was powerless over this addiction and that I needed divine strength. That day, I told my wife what I'd done (that I'd quit drinking) and I confessed how bad things had truly become. It was an uncomfortable and humbling conversation, but it was also the first step toward honesty and healing.

That same week, I visited my doctor and sought professional help for my depression and withdrawal symptoms. I began seeing a psychiatrist and a Christian counsellor, who helped me unpack the underlying issues: the various sources of my depression, anxiety, and addiction, like unresolved grief and chronic stress.

With their help, I started to develop healthier coping strategies. It was an arduous journey; those early days of sobriety were filled with intense cravings, mood swings, and the temptation to go back to the bottle. But by God's grace and with support, I stayed the course one day at a time.

I also confided in a few close friends and mentors, both inside and outside my church, who could hold me accountable and encourage me without judgment.

Quitting alcohol was a huge victory, but it didn't solve everything overnight. I was sober, yes, but I was still wrestling with depression and anxiety. For years after 2005, I maintained my sobriety yet continued to keep my depression hidden like a dark and shameful secret.

I was dry, but not truly free in an emotional and spiritual sense. I still felt that stigma, shame, and fear about my mental health struggles. It took another turning point, over a decade later, for me to experience a deeper freedom.

That moment came in a seminary classroom of all places. I remember the day clearly. I was a theology professor at the time, teaching a class on being open and vulnerable in pastoral ministry. In the middle of the lecture, I felt a gentle but firm nudge in my heart: "But you're not open and honest about your struggles. How is keeping this secret helping you or my church?"

It was the Holy Spirit speaking to me. I stopped mid-sentence, took a deep breath, and began to share with my students what I'd never shared publicly before: my story of battling depression and alcohol abuse.

I told them about my years of silent suffering and the journey I'd begun toward recovery. I was trembling, afraid of what they might think, but I couldn't preach vulnerability and continue to wear a mask.

To my amazement, I was met not with judgment but with love, understanding, and support. After class, several students came up to me, hugged me, and even confided their struggles with depression and addiction, which they'd never dared to share.

That day, something broke loose in me. The shame lost its power. By stepping into the light, I experienced an overwhelming sense of relief and a profound sense of God's grace. I began to see that being honest about my pain could help others start "the journey toward healing and recovery," just as it was helping me heal more deeply.

## Faith, Family, and the Journey to Wholeness

Through these turning points, I learned that recovery isn't a solo journey (nor merely a physical one) but a holistic path involving God and community.

My faith in Jesus Christ became the bedrock of my recovery, especially as I confronted the underlying depression. I came to believe in a new way that God's love for me wasn't dependent on my life being perfectly together. In fact, amid my brokenness, I encountered Christ's grace more profoundly than ever.

Scripture's promises of forgiveness and new creation took on a very personal meaning. I clung to verses about God being near to the broken-hearted. In prayer, I often felt God assuring me, "I'm here. We'll walk out of this valley together."

Indeed, I could allow those seasons of difficulty to drive me toward my ultimate source of recovery, comfort, healing, hope, and strength: Jesus Christ. I also realized that God works through healthcare professionals in the recovery process. My therapists, doctors, and support group were gifts from God, guiding me toward wholeness. Recovery required both prayer and therapy, as well as faith and medicine. There was no shame in utilizing all the tools God was providing.

My family played a crucial role as well. My wife showed incredible patience and support, especially once I opened up about my struggles. She prayed for me and encouraged me daily to stay sober. Addiction professionals told her to give up on me, because I'd never stop drinking, given my addiction history. But she refused to give up and stood by me through my recovery, often at significant cost to herself. Her courage, patience, and character are astonishing, and I'll be forever grateful to her.

My children, in their way, gave me hope for the future: I wanted to become the healthy father they deserved. I also can't overstate the importance of the wider church community in my healing. When I finally shared my story with a few trusted colleagues and later with my church, I discovered an outpouring of compassion.

The ministry team of my local church stood by me and my family, caring for us during my greatest struggles. They didn't cast me aside; instead, they walked with me, checking in on my well-being and covering my responsibilities when I needed rest. Their love and support made a huge difference to my recovery.

This showed me what the church can be at its best: a safe, healing, forgiving, loving, embracing, and vulnerable community that helps people find hope and freedom. If any one of them had shamed me or rejected me, I might have retreated into silence.

But their grace gave me the courage to continue in honesty. It also taught me that I wasn't alone; there were others in the pews struggling with similar issues, quietly longing for someone to say, "Me too. Let's get through this together."

Another significant part of my faith journey was learning to accept myself as a person in recovery, not a failure. I had to internalize that my identity is in Christ, not in my past addiction. Yes, I'm someone who dealt with alcoholism and depression, but I'm also a beloved child of God.

Over time, I found purpose in my pain. I sensed God calling me to use my story to encourage others. I discovered the power of opening up and telling my story: it brings healing for me and offers hope to others who are still struggling. This realization transformed my perspective on my past. Rather than seeing it as a shameful secret, I began to see it as a testimony of God's grace and deliverance.

## Staying Free: Daily Practices of a New Life

Recovery isn't a one-time event: It's a continual process, a daily choice to live in the light. By God's grace, I have remained alcohol-free since 2005. On July 23, 2025, I celebrated twenty years sober! That's only possible by the grace of God and the love of family and friends. To maintain my freedom, I had to replace old, destructive habits with new, life-giving ones.

I became very intentional about developing my emotional, relational, and spiritual resources so that I could flourish without needing to numb myself. In practical terms, that means I built a sustainable rhythm of healthy practices and boundaries that guard my wellbeing. Some of the key practices that help keep me free from alcohol and addiction include:

### Daily Spiritual Disciplines

I foster a vital relationship with God through devotional reading and prayer. Every morning, I spend time reading Scripture or uplifting books and meditating on God's promises. Prayer has become my lifeline: I honestly tell God how I'm feeling, and I draw strength and comfort from divine presence. My daily practice involves engaging in Lectio Divina prayers in the morning and Examen prayers in the evening.[1] These habits center me and give me hope each day.

### Mentoring and Accountability

I meet regularly with a spiritual director, a Christian mentor, a professional supervisor, a Christian counselor, and a small group of trusted friends. That's a lot of relationships, but I've found these essential to my emotional,

1. For Lectio Divina, see *Rule of St. Benedict*, ch. 48; for the Examen, see Ignatius of Loyola, *Spiritual Exercises*, §§43–54.

psychological, and spiritual well-being, and my freedom from addiction. In those meetings, I remain open and vulnerable about my struggles: nothing is kept in the dark. They ask me the hard questions about how I'm doing. This accountability and encouragement are crucial. As I often say now, I'm no longer afraid to talk about my experiences and struggles. Keeping that honesty prevents secrets or new addictions from taking root.

## Exercise and Recreation

I learned that caring for my body is a key part of caring for my soul. I go on daily walks with my Golden Retriever, and I picked up swimming at the beach: Physical activity relieves stress and improves my mood tremendously. I also make time for recreation and hobbies I enjoy, like reading novels, building Lego sets, and spending time in nature. These bring balance and joy to my life, where I once lived solely to work (and then drink).

## Therapy and Self-Care

I continue to see a therapist periodically (a Christian psychologist), especially during challenging seasons, to help me process any new issues that arise. I practice self-care by getting adequate rest (avoiding late nights of work and drinking), maintaining a healthy diet, and recognizing my emotional triggers. If I notice signs of depression or anxiety returning, I reach out for help immediately: I now know where to go to get help when I need it.

## Helping Others

Perhaps one of the most fulfilling practices is helping others who struggle with addiction or mental health issues. I openly share my testimony in churches, classes, men's and women's groups, addiction gatherings, podcasts, and conversations, not to boast, but to break the stigma and let people know they're not alone. In doing so, I have found that sharing my recovery story isn't only healing for me but also for others. It reminds me how far I've come and reinforces my commitment to never return to that darkness. It's incredible to see how God can redeem my past by using it to guide someone else toward freedom.

Each of these practices is part of a holistic lifestyle of recovery.[2] There's no point at which I can say, "I'm cured, I can let my guard down now." I

2. May, *Addiction and Grace*.

remain vigilant, but not fearful. I know I'm not fighting alone. I rely daily on God's grace to sustain me. Whenever I face stress or sadness now, I have healthier outlets and a supportive network to lean on. And I continue to dwell in God's promises, which give me hope and purpose.

## A New Chapter of Freedom and Purpose

Today, I'm living in freedom. It's the freedom of being unashamed and unafraid to be honest about who I am: a man who has struggled, who has fallen, but who has also been redeemed and renewed.

It's the freedom of no longer needing a substance to get through the day, and the freedom of experiencing joy and peace in sobriety. My depression, while still present at times, no longer defines me; it's something I manage with God's help, not a dark secret that controls me.

Writing this account as if it were a chapter in my memoir, I feel immense gratitude. I'm grateful to God, who never gave up on me and gently led me back into the light. I'm thankful to my family and friends, who "stood by me" in love even at my worst. I'm grateful for the church communities that embraced me and allowed me to heal rather than condemning me.

And I'm grateful for the second chance at life that recovery has given me: the chance to see my daughters grow up, to continue serving in ministry, and to walk alongside others in their pain.

If there's one message I hope my story conveys, it's this: You don't need to feel condemned or ashamed when you struggle. There is hope and help available. For me, that hope was ultimately found in Jesus and in the loving community he surrounded me with.

No matter how dark or hopeless things seem, freedom is possible. I found it by taking the courageous steps of honesty, reaching out for help, and trusting God one day at a time. My journey to freedom from alcohol and addiction has been the hardest thing I've ever done, but also the most rewarding.

In place of despair, I have hope. In place of secrecy, I have authenticity. And in place of addiction, I have purpose. Sharing this story is part of that purpose: a testament to the reality and worth of recovery. I'm living proof that a person can struggle mightily and yet, with support and faith, emerge into a life of wholeness and freedom. All thanks be to God for this journey of grace.

# Introduction

## The Crisis of Addiction and Hope of Freedom

THERE'S A LONGING WRITTEN into the marrow of every soul. This yearning is a deep, aching hunger for freedom, wholeness, and peace. Yet so many wander through life bound by chains they never intended to wear, stumbling under burdens they don't know how to lay down.

Addiction is one of the cruelest of these chains. It strangles hope, distorts love, and leaves hearts exiled from joy. But even here, in the shadowed valleys of bondage, grace waits. This is a book for those who dare to believe that no darkness is too thick for light to pierce and no prison so strong that God can't break its bars.

### The Bondage of Addiction and the Need for Hope

Addiction sweeps through our world like a silent tempest, tearing through individuals, families, and entire communities. Its devastation isn't confined to crumpled bodies, broken families, or empty bank accounts. It scars the human soul. In every darkened room where someone hides with a bottle or a needle or a glowing screen, there echoes a primal ache: "How did I become so enslaved?" Addiction is more than a neurochemical snare. It's a profound spiritual crisis: a distortion of desire, a restless groping for transcendence in things that can never satisfy.

This crisis reaches far beyond private pain. Families fracture under the weight of secrets. Children carry invisible wounds from watching a parent disappear into substances or screens. Marriages falter, friendships fade, and communities shoulder rising tides of crime, poverty, suicide, and despair. The world throws numbers at us: billions lost in productivity, millions dead from overdoses, countless lives shortened by alcohol, tobacco, and sedatives. But behind every statistic is a beloved image-bearer of God, hunched beneath shame, haunted by regret, desperate to be made whole.

At its heart, addiction reveals a sacred longing gone awry. Underneath the compulsion lies a holy hunger: a yearning for communion, meaning, love, freedom, and peace. The tragedy is that many reach for false absolutions. They chase fleeting highs, hoping to quiet an ache that's spiritual at its core. Addiction isn't merely a medical or psychological issue (though it's certainly that); it's also a spiritual captivity.[1] The person enslaved by addiction cries out for deliverance, often without knowing to whom they cry.

This is why hope isn't optional. Hope is the lifeline thrown into the storm. Without hope, recovery collapses under the gravity of despair. Without hope, shame festers and whispers that change is impossible. Yet hope (rooted in something far more profound than mere optimism) is precisely what faith offers. A spiritual perspective refuses to treat the person with an addiction as a lost cause or a hopeless case. It dares to say that no pit's so bottomless that grace can't reach deeper still. It dares to see chains broken and lives redeemed.

This book begins here: at the intersection of raw human bondage and divine promise. It insists that the crisis of addiction is ultimately a question of the heart's orientation, the soul's disordered loves. And it declares that there is One who still sets captives free, who binds up the brokenhearted, who trades ashes for beauty, who offers dignity in the place of shame, and who loves completely and unconditionally.[2] In the rubble of addiction, seeds of resurrection can yet take root. And that's why we must press on: because under the wreckage, hope breathes.

## Beyond Self-Help: Why Spirituality Matters

Countless people embark on the road to recovery armed with sheer grit. They muster willpower, clutch twelve-step pamphlets, download apps, attend therapy sessions, and recite affirmations. And make no mistake, these tools matter. They often save lives. Therapy is a gift. Rehabilitation programs provide crucial scaffolding. Medications can stabilize, and support groups can sustain. But to imagine that addiction can be vanquished by human effort alone is to misunderstand the depths of its reach. For addiction seeps into the very marrow of the spirit. It isn't simply a behavioral glitch to be reprogrammed; it's a deep wound in the soul's fabric.

1. See Augustine, *Confessions*, 3.8, on the concept of disordered loves.
2. See Isa 61:1–3; Luke 4:18–19.

Underneath the compulsions and cravings often lies a cavernous void; an aching emptiness born of disconnection from the Source of all life. Many who battle addiction carry silent histories of trauma, rejection, or profound loneliness. Their drug of choice becomes a counterfeit sacrament: an attempt to soothe what only divine love can truly heal. Addiction becomes a misdirected liturgy, a ritual that promises transcendence but delivers ruin.[3] This is why countless people "white-knuckle" sobriety only to relapse: the deeper hunger was never addressed. The heart was never reoriented toward a truer Love.

A purely secular recovery plan can curb the behavior, but often leaves the soul gasping. This book, therefore, contends for a hybrid approach. It holds together the necessity of practical recovery strategies (therapy, accountability, reorienting thoughts, and lifestyle change) with the indispensable power of Christian spirituality. Because only when the soul encounters the living God does the restless ache find rest. Only then does forgiveness wash over guilt, grace uproot shame, and hope displace despair. Only then does a person discover that they aren't merely a bundle of impulses to be managed, but a beloved child called by name, destined for communion.

This spiritual approach isn't a naïve bypass of psychological realities. It isn't a simplistic "just pray more" solution. Instead, it's an acknowledgment that humans are embodied souls.[4] Lasting transformation requires touching every layer of who we are: physical, emotional, psychological, relational, and spiritual. True freedom is never achieved by external compliance alone. Our liberation emerges from a heart remade by grace.

So, this journey invites readers beyond self-help into sacred surrender. It beckons them to lay down self-reliance and receive a power not their own. For in the end, the truest recovery story isn't just about conquering addiction; it's about being found, embraced, and made new by a Love deeper than any craving. This is why spirituality matters: not as decoration on top of recovery, but as its beating heart.

## A Journey of Faith and Transformation

This book is an invitation to journey from desolation to renewal, from the ash heaps of addiction to the green fields of wholeness. I don't promise an easy path, nor a swift one, for the soul is tender ground and deep roots take time to heal. Freedom from addiction was a long and challenging journey

3. See Smith, *Desiring the Kingdom*, 23–30, on Smith's notion that we are liturgical creatures shaped by rival "secular liturgies."

4. May, *Addiction and Grace*, 3–7.

for me. But I can promise that with each honest step, guided by grace, there is hope of becoming truly free.

We'll walk together through stages that mirror both the rugged honesty of recovery and the luminous way of discipleship. The first stretch of the road is a place of hard reckoning: an unflinching self-examination that refuses to dress up our wounds or make excuses for our chains. It's here, in the dim mirror of truth, that many first glimpse both their desperate need and the flicker of something more. The invitation is to stop hiding, to stand naked before God's searching light, and to confess what already aches inside.

From there, we move into surrender. Not the clenched-fist surrender of someone forced to give up a fight, but the tear-streaked, humility-soaked, holy yielding of one who has been loved into letting go. We lay down the illusion of control. We open trembling hands to Jesus Christ, saying, "Take all of me: my failures, my trauma, my story, my cravings, my shame, and my fragile hopes." This isn't a single moment but a continual posture, a thousand small deaths to old ways that slowly give birth to life.

Renewing the mind is next. Addiction carves grooves of distortion into our thoughts, rehearsing lies of worthlessness, despair, entitlement, or invincibility. Scripture becomes both sword and salve here. By soaking in truth (truth about who God is, who we are, and how broken, vulnerable, loved, and precious we are), we begin to rewrite the narratives that once kept us ensnared. Meditation on divine promises replaces the endless echo of addiction's deceit.

Forgiveness is a stream that runs through the entire journey. It may mean seeking forgiveness from others we have wounded, or it may mean daring to accept forgiveness from God when we feel least deserving. It's also learning to extend grace to ourselves: receiving the reality that we're more than our worst choices. In forgiving, we unclench our hands from the stones we have long carried, stones meant for our heads.

Finally, we look toward building a new life. Not simply abstaining from an old habit, but constructing fresh rhythms that nurture body, mind, and spirit. This includes cultivating joy, reweaving community, discovering purpose beyond self, and embedding practices that keep us close to the heart of God. It's the slow art of crafting a life that no longer needs to flee into false comfort.

Each step in this journey blends timeless biblical wisdom with practical insights from the best of recovery practice. It's about learning to walk by the Spirit in the daily grind of temptation and stress. It's about discovering that even relapse isn't the end of hope, but often another grace-soaked lesson in humility and resilience.

Above all, this is a path walked together: with God and with others. No one is expected to wander this wilderness alone. And so, if you feel too broken, too far gone, and too ashamed, know this: You are precisely the one this journey is meant for. Grace has always specialized in meeting us in our wilderness and leading us home.

## Christ-Centered and Grounded in Bible and Theology

This book isn't a generic self-help manual dressed up with spiritual jargon. It's unashamedly, deeply Christian: rooted in Scripture, anchored in historic theology, grounded in ancient spiritual and discipleship practices, and propelled by the living, empowering presence of Jesus Christ. Its pages breathe with the ancient conviction that addiction isn't merely a habit to be broken, but evidence of hearts estranged from their true center.

Christian theology dares to diagnose addiction at its deepest level: as disordered love, as sin and captivity that flow from humanity's primordial rupture with God.[5] Our compulsions expose how desperately we long to fill the void that only divine communion can satisfy. Whether it's alcohol, porn, work, illicit drugs, gambling, or endless scrolling, these become our idols, our golden calves built in the shadow of Sinai while we wait for a God we fear will never come down.[6] They promise transcendence and deliver chains; they offer escape and deliver bondage.

Yet the same theology that soberly names sin also erupts with good news. It declares that we aren't left to rot in Egypt's mud pits. The story of Scripture is the story of a God who parts seas to liberate captives, who descends into our dust to lift us out, who takes on flesh to walk through death so we might walk free. In Christ, addiction's deepest bonds are shattered at the cross, and new life is possible through resurrection. Redemption isn't theoretical; it's blood-won, embodied, offered without cost yet at infinite cost.[7]

In this book, I linger extensively on themes like grace and forgiveness, because the addicted soul is often tormented by self-hatred. I explore sanctification: the Spirit's slow, patient work of making us new.[8] I highlight the church not as a judgmental gallery but as a hospital for the sin-sick, a community meant to bandage wounds and bear burdens together.[9]

5. Augustine, *Confessions*, 3.8.
6. See Exod 32:1–6.
7. See Eph 1:7; Heb 9:12.
8. Calvin, *Institutes of the Christian Religion*, 3.3.
9. Luther, "Lectures on Galatians," 356.

I ground our understanding of recovery in profound biblical metaphors: being born again, putting off the old self, abiding in the vine, experiencing death and resurrection, and walking in the light. These aren't quaint religious slogans; they're the spiritual architecture of transformation. The living word is sharper than any scalpel, cutting away rot so new flesh might grow.

By weaving theology and Scripture through every chapter, this book invites you not just to quit a destructive behavior but to embrace a whole new way of being, to become rooted in a love that satisfies the deepest hungers, that welcomes prodigals without scolding, that clothes the shamed and lifts the fallen. In these pages, we'll trace how God's story reframes our story, turning sites of ruin into altars of praise.

So come as you are (addicted, angry, afraid, ashamed, and half-believing), and find in these truths a place to start again. The gospel is wide enough for your failures and strong enough for your cravings. Let theology do its holy work: dismantling your idols, remaking your desires, and setting you free for joy.

## My Approach in This Book

I write these pages not as a clinical expert in addiction medicine or as a credentialed psychologist, but as one who knows firsthand the painful, terrible contours of bondage and the fierce, patient mercy that leads us out. My story involved years of wrestling with alcohol and depression, seasons where I all but drowned beneath shame and silence. It was there, in that hushed and desolate space, that I discovered the God who descends into dark valleys, who doesn't recoil from messy stories, and who stitches new garments out of tatters.

My background is in Christian spirituality and theology. I've spent decades studying the deep wells of Scripture, church history, spiritual practices, and contemplative life. I've taught seminarians and pastors, preached in sanctuaries, and sat by countless souls unraveling in sorrow or sin. Yet all this learning would ring hollow if it didn't speak to the raw edges of human ache and desire. This book emerges from the crucible of my brokenness, tempered by the extended schooling of grace. It's a book written by a writer-theologian who has stumbled out of hidden rooms reeking of despair into the unexpected sunlight of freedom.

So, I offer this work not as a specialist who diagnoses disorders, prescribes medication, or charts clinical recovery plans. Those roles are sacred and necessary, and I honor the women and men who serve in them. Many need therapy, medical care, and structured programs to heal (as I have so often), and there's no shame in that. I urge it. But my calling is different. I come alongside as a spiritual guide, a fellow pilgrim who knows what it means to limp toward wholeness. I write as a Christian mentor, a soul friend, and someone who has traced addiction's claw marks across their spirit and still bears witness to resurrection.

I take a spiritual and theological approach because I believe addiction is, at its core, not merely a chemical dependency or psychological compulsion (though it's surely both) but also a wound in the soul, a distortion of love, a hunger misdirected. The ancient Christian tradition speaks profoundly to these realities. It names our disordered attachments, confronts our idols, calls us to repentance and restoration, and anchors us in the radical assurance that no one is beyond the reach of grace.[10]

Throughout these pages, I won't pretend to be what I'm not. I won't offer diagnostic categories or medical prescriptions. Instead, I'll offer something else: an invitation to look beneath the surface, to discern the deeper longings that addiction mimics, and to discover how the God who binds up the brokenhearted might bind up yours. I'll point toward ancient paths of prayer, Scripture, confession, community, and surrender, because these are the ways I found breath again when my chest was crushed by darkness. I stand here simply as one pilgrim telling another where bread might be found and how the narrow path of discipleship to Jesus offers grace, freedom, dignity, and hope.

## Hope and the Promise of Freedom

If all this book offered were an analysis of addiction's devastation (its theft of dignity, its hollowing of relationships, its immersion in secrecy and shame, and its heavy toll on mind and body), it would leave us crushed beneath the weight of despair. But that's not the final word. The final word is hope, fierce and unyielding. Hope that doesn't arise from naive optimism or shallow slogans, but from the deep reservoirs of God's promises and character. Hope that's anchored in the unshakeable declaration that Christ has come to set captives free.

"It's for freedom that Christ has set us free," the apostle Paul writes, as if to remind us that liberation isn't a side benefit of the gospel but its blazing center.[11] And again, Jesus promises, "If the Son sets you free, you will be free indeed": not halfway free, not tenuously free, but wholly, joyously,

10. Augustine, *Confessions*, 3.8; see also *City of God*, 19.13.

11. Gal 5:1.

enduringly free.[12] These aren't theoretical aspirations; they're Christ's blood-won certainties, sealed by a cross and an empty tomb.

I've lived long enough inside the grip of addiction to know how hollow such words can sound when you are still shackled. I've also lived long enough outside it to know they're truer than any lie addiction ever uttered. For the same power that spoke galaxies into being and rose Jesus Christ from the dead is the power that can untangle the knots of compulsion within a human heart. The same Spirit that hovered over chaos in the beginning hovers still over our chaos, ready to birth new creation and fullness of life.[13]

I write this book with the stubborn expectancy that no person is beyond God's rescue. It doesn't matter how many times you've fallen, how deep the pit, how long you've been circling the same weary cycles. Divine mercy isn't exhausted by your failures. Grace has never been stingy. The arms of God remain open, especially to those most convinced they have forfeited all welcome.

So let this be your hope as you turn these pages: that through them, and far beyond them, God might speak to you. That old lies might lose their grip. That places long dead within you might stir with life. That wounds you thought would never close might become scars telling stories of healing. That you might taste the astonishing freedom of walking unchained.

No journey is without setbacks. No soul emerges from deep bondage without trembling. But the God who has called you is faithful. And if you dare to take even faltering steps toward the light, you may yet find that chains fall, that shame dissipates, and that your life becomes a living testimony to this breathtaking promise: whom the Son sets free is free indeed.[14]

So, linger here for a sacred moment. Let your restless heart feel the weight of this longing and this hunger: the chains that still cling, the hollow places that ache for communion, the yearning that has never quite been silenced. And then dare to believe that even here, in these shadowed valleys, a Love deeper than your bondage waits to lift your head, untangle your sorrows, and say, "There is more. There is freedom yet for you." Pause, breathe, and let hope rise.

12. John 8:36.

13. Gen 1:2; Rom 8:11.

14. John 8:36.

## Reflection Questions

1. Where have I seen the signs of addiction or bondage in my life: whether to substances, habits, or inner patterns?
2. What longings or wounds have I tried to numb or escape through those behaviors?
3. How do I respond to the idea that addiction is both a spiritual crisis and a cry for healing?
4. What gives me hope that change is possible?
5. What might it look like to begin a journey from shame to freedom?

## Action Steps

1. Write a one-page letter to yourself describing your desire for freedom, honesty, and healing.
2. Share with a trusted friend, pastor, or mentor that you're beginning this journey.
3. Choose a Scripture that speaks to your hope for change (e.g., Isa 43:18–19 or John 8:36). Memorize it this week.
4. Begin a simple daily practice: two minutes of silence, followed by this prayer: "God, I'm here. I need you. Lead me toward freedom."

# 1.

# Recognizing the Need for Help and God's Grace

There comes a moment when our soul grows weary of its chains, when the yearning to be whole becomes louder than the lies that keep us bound. This is sacred ground, where truth begins to dawn, and grace stands ready to take our hand.

## The Reality of Addiction's Grip

Addiction isn't a casual vice, a private quirk, or a mere slip of self-control. It's a tyrant that worms its way into the inner sanctums of the heart, planting its flag on territory that was meant to be sacred. It reshapes appetites, rewires instincts, commandeers affections, and infiltrates relationships. It nudges in dark hours, promising relief, promising a hush to the endless ache, promising escape from the pain. And for a fleeting moment, it delivers: a sedative veil, a counterfeit balm, a momentary distraction. But then it demands payment with interest. Soon, what began as comfort becomes a cage.

The person ensnared by addiction finds thoughts orbiting obsessively around the next indulgence, behaviors bending inevitably toward securing the fix, decisions increasingly dictated by the need to quiet a craving that grows ever louder. Entire lives become structured around this pursuit. I couldn't go a couple of hours without a drink of alcohol, and when I wasn't drinking, thoughts about needing alcohol were ever-present. Relationships are sacrificed on its altar. Integrity is chipped away in small dishonesties that accumulate into a hollowness of character. Physical health wilts under the weight of repeated abuse. And beneath it all, the soul becomes thin, afraid, ashamed, stretched, and haunted by a gnawing awareness of bondage.

It's common to hear people say, "Why don't they just stop?" When someone says that, they're assuming addiction is simply a matter of willpower, a moral laziness easily overcome by grit. But those who have lived under its regime know better. Addiction is a potent cocktail of neurochemical dependence, psychological escape, relational codependence, and spiritual vacuum. It hijacks dopamine pathways, but also becomes an emotional refuge, a false lover, and a shield against wounds too tender to face sober. Addiction mimics sacrament, promising transcendence, ritual, freedom, and belonging. This is why addiction is so cruel: It knows exactly where to place its claws.

And so, the addicted person often wakes to moments of sobering terror: standing in the wreckage of another relapse, catching a glimpse of what they've become. They may swear off the substance or behavior, may vow with tears to do better, and may ask their closest relationships to forgive and believe their promises. But the grip is deep, the longing lurks, and the cage feels impossible to overcome. Days pass, the ache returns, and the cycle tightens. This is why addiction is more than a bad habit. It's a form of slavery, an idolatrous devotion to something that can't save, a cruel master that extracts more than it ever gives.[1]

If you see yourself here, know this: You aren't uniquely broken. You aren't alone in feeling powerless. I've been there too, and millions stand with you in this haunted valley. More importantly, there's a Good Shepherd who walks among the shattered to lead them home. But the first step is to name the bondage for what it's and to stop calling chains by softer names.

## Breaking Through Denial

Denial is addiction's most cunning ally. It dresses in gentle tones: "It's just stress relief. Everyone needs something. I'm not doing this more than others I know. I can stop whenever I want." It rationalizes with half-truths: "At least it's not as bad as what others do. It's under control." It minimizes with a dismissive shrug: "I deserve this. It's no one's business but mine." And in our mind, these lies sound convincing.

Denial is a fog that protects the addiction, shielding it from scrutiny, insulating it from the hard light of truth, enabling the behaviors to continue. Denial promises that tomorrow will be different, that today's excess was warranted by a hard week, that the damage done is minimal and easily

1. See John 8:34; Rom 6:16; also Exod 20:3–5 for idolatry as misplaced worship.

repaired. Meanwhile, slowly, inevitably, the roots drive deeper. Relationships become strained under the unspoken weight of secrets. Finances crumble under hidden expenditures. Health declines in small, sinister increments. The heart loses faith in its value and integrity. The soul grows more anxious, more defensive, more brittle. But the person wrapped in denial doesn't (or can't) see it. It's easier to keep telling the story that nothing is wrong.

Yet every truly healed life begins in the same place: with truth. Jesus said, "You will know the truth, and the truth will set you free."[2] Not coddling, not pretending, not excusing, not avoiding. Freedom is born in candor. Liberty arrives with the light. The truth is that addiction has likely taken more than you dare to admit. It may have stolen nights of sleep, laughter that once came easily, intimacy that once felt safe, trust that once was whole. It may have left you making choices you swore you never would, telling lies you never imagined yourself speaking.

So, pause here. Ask yourself hard questions. When was the last day you went without your substance or behavior? How much of your thought life does it occupy? Who have you kept in the dark? How often do you hide your behaviors with lies and half-truths? What do you fear would happen if you stopped? If you find excuses rushing to the surface, gently push them aside and look again. Living in truth is painful at first, like emerging from a darkened theatre into glaring noon light. But it's also a profound mercy. For denial keeps us imprisoned, while honesty opens the first crack in the cell door.

To acknowledge, "I have a problem. I'm not in control. I need help," is no small admission. It's a spiritual milestone. It's the crossing of a threshold where grace stands waiting. The God who delights in truth in the inward being draws near to the heart that lays bare.[3] Healing doesn't begin with perfection; it starts with honesty. If you can stand courageously in that truth today, you're already on holy ground. The rest will follow by grace.

## Counting the Cost

There's a necessary sorrow in pausing long enough to take stock of what addiction has stolen. Many rush past this reckoning, eager to reach hope without sitting among the ruins. But truth demands we linger here and look closely, courageously, and honestly. Otherwise, how can we genuinely long for freedom if we aren't fully awake to the tyranny that has ruled our lives through addiction?

2. John 8:32.

3. Ps 51:6.

Consider your body first. How many nights have you spent restless or sick, your body groaning under the weight of chemicals, stress, or sleepless obsession? Has your skin grown dull, your energy sapped, your eyes strained, your health compromised by choices made to feed a craving? Then look at the mind. Anxiety, fog, shame, grief, anger, depression, and racing thoughts at night that never let you rest: all often worsened by the very thing you clutch for comfort.

Now turn to the heart of it: your relationships. How many moments with family slipped by unnoticed because you were preoccupied or absent in spirit? How many friends drifted away, wearied by broken promises or wounded by sharp words uttered under the influence? How many times did your children or partner catch a hollow look in your eyes, seeing you there, but not truly there?

Trace the lines further. What about your work? Your finances? Addiction is a costly master. Missed opportunities, mounting debt, reputation frayed by unreliability—all these tally silently; they take their toll slowly but surely. And still deeper: what of your soul? The distance felt from God, the shame and sharp pain when you try to pray, the hollow echo in worship, the Bible left unopened, not because you don't believe it true, but because facing it feels like facing a mirror you can't bear.

This self-examination isn't about drowning you in guilt. It's about opening your eyes wide to reality so you might grasp why freedom matters. Try this humble but brave exercise: Take pen and paper, write down how your addiction has harmed your body, mind, relationships, work, finances, and spiritual life. Be painfully specific. Then look at those pages not to condemn yourself, but to clarify why this journey matters. Every line written is a sacred cry for redemption. Every loss is ground God longs to reclaim.

Change is rarely born of abstract conviction; it's kindled by honest grief. To count the cost is to permit yourself to mourn, and in that mourning to find holy motivation.[4] When you do this, you'll see just how much there is to recover, restore, and rebuild. Grace waits on the other side of truth.

## The Spiritual Void Beneath the Addiction

If we peel back all the tangled layers of addiction (the biology, the trauma, the habit loops, the social pressures), we find beneath it a restless emptiness. A spiritual vacuum. A cavernous longing that has tried to sate itself on things that can't fill.

4. See Nouwen, *Inner Voice of Love*, on grief and transformation.

For many, the substance or behavior first arrived like a tender mercy. A salve to numb old wounds, a shield against unbearable loneliness, a hush over a mind that wouldn't quiet. It seemed to promise rest, transcendence, peace, relief. But what began as a borrowed comfort soon became an insatiable god with cruel appetites, demanding constant sacrifice. The drink, the high, the screen, the work, the sexual rush: they all offered fleeting sanctuaries that demanded worship, sacrifices, and secrecy. Addiction isn't just a disorder of the brain; it's a disordered love. It's, at its core, misplaced worship.[5]

This is why people find themselves returning repeatedly to what they know will wound them, because something in us is driven to seek joy, belonging, and meaning. When these hungers go unmet at the level of the soul, we grasp at shadows. As Augustine so piercingly confessed, "Our hearts are restless until they rest in you, O Lord."[6] And every relapse, every private binge, every promise to ourselves that "this will be the last time," is often nothing more than the soul's desperate groping for the holy and loving in places they can't be found.

To see addiction this way isn't to excuse it. But it does reframe the struggle. It reveals that beneath the compulsion lies a sacred longing: a yearning for communion, for peace, for an embrace that tells us we're deeply loved and eternally safe. Your addiction isn't proof of how hopelessly corrupt you are; it's tragic evidence of how profoundly you long for something real, intimate, divine, and sustaining.

Only God can fill that void. Only God's love (not as abstract doctrine but as a living encounter) can satisfy the heart's deepest thirst. The lie of addiction is that it can offer what only God can give: comfort for wounds, assurance in chaos, intimacy for loneliness, and pleasure that doesn't rot into regret. When we begin to see our struggle as a misplaced attempt to satisfy a spiritual hunger, we can stop simply trying to manage symptoms and start reaching for the true feast.

So, pause and let this truth sink into every restless corner of your heart: your cravings aren't merely shameful impulses; they're distorted echoes of a deeper desire to be known, to be healed, to be safe, to be free, and to be held. And in that deeper desire, God is already moving to meet you.

5. See Augustine, *Confessions*, esp. 2.2; and the theological tradition on *ordo amoris*.

6. Augustine, *Confessions*, 1.1.

## Admitting Powerlessness Is the First Step

There's a profound grace that lives in rock bottom. It's the grace of coming to the end of yourself. No more excuses. No more grand promises to change next week. No more pretending that willpower is enough. No more believing you can be free independently and in your strength alone. Just the raw, honest, vulnerable confession that echoes through the deepest valleys: *I can't do this anymore.* And that cry, though it may sound like defeat, is the doorway to deliverance.

This is the first step of every true recovery journey: admitting we're powerless.[7] In recovery language, it's the honest recognition that addiction has become unmanageable.[8] In Christian spirituality, it's the humble acknowledgment that apart from the vine, the branch withers (John 15:5). We need help (human and divine) to be free and recover. Our strength can't carry the weight of our healing. Our clever strategies can't conquer the cravings. We can't heal our own wounds with the same hands that keep reopening them.

Unless we reach the point of acknowledging our addiction and accepting our powerlessness to change without help, we won't change and get free. Many people never reach this first step. But those who do take one of the most significant strides in recovery and liberation from addiction.

And yet, this is no counsel of despair. It's the Spirit's call to surrender. The illusion of control is the first idol that must fall. Pride says, *I've got this.* Grace replies, *Let go.* For the humble heart becomes fertile ground for divine help. "God opposes the proud but gives grace to the humble" (Jas 4:6). Powerlessness, when brought into the light, becomes sacred soil in which new strength can grow.

This isn't passivity. It's not a shrug of resignation. It's a holy yielding, a surrender with fire in its bones. It's raising empty hands and saying, *If I'm to be free, I'll need a power far greater than myself. I'll need mercy. I'll need Presence. I'll need God.* And in that prayer, spoken in weakness and surrender, everything begins to change. God reveals divine power in our weakness, vulnerability, dependence, and surrender.

Here's the paradox at the heart of transformation: only those who confess their need can be filled. Only those who fall to their knees can be

7. White, *Slaying the Dragon*; Maté, *In the Realm of Hungry Ghosts*; Hazelden Betty Ford Foundation, "Twelve Steps of Alcoholics Anonymous."

8. Step 1 of the Alcoholics Anonymous Twelve Steps reads, "We admitted we were powerless over alcohol: that our lives had become unmanageable." Alcoholics Anonymous, *Alcoholics Anonymous*, 59.

lifted. Your admission of helplessness isn't the end of your story—it's the beginning of it. Powerlessness isn't your prison; it's your passage into grace.

## Understanding Sin and Brokenness

Addiction isn't simply a problem to solve. It's a mirror to the human condition; a manifestation of the ancient yearning and fallenness that lives in every heart. In the depths of our hearts, there's an ache that longs to be loved, to be whole, to be forgiven, to be free, to be seen, to be healed, and to be saved. The Bible calls this condition *sin*: not merely in the sense of wrongdoing, but as the fundamental disorientation of our lives away from God and toward lesser gods that can't save.

We are, all of us, prone to wander. We carve idols out of pleasure, comfort, desire, control, or success. We bow to them daily, often unconsciously. And in addiction, those idols become tyrants. The drink, the pill, the shopping, the food, the work, the dopamine hit, the secret screen: all begin as promises of peace. But they don't give peace. They demand sacrifice. And soon, what was once a choice becomes a chain.

Romans 6:16 says it plainly: "You are slaves of the one you obey." This is the spiritual gravity of addiction. What you give your heart to, you eventually serve. And what you serve, if not rooted in love and truth, will consume you. Addiction, then, isn't merely a behavioral glitch; it's a form of spiritual captivity. It's the fruit of a more profound brokenness, a distortion of worship. The substance becomes a false savior. The behavior becomes a counterfeit blessing. And the soul grows hollow and thinner.

But this must be said with care: to speak of sin and brokenness isn't to shame. We all suffer the same illness and need human and divine help. To sin and experience brokenness is to be human. To talk of sin and suffering is to name the truth, and in naming it, to make healing possible. Jesus didn't come to applaud the self-sufficient. He came to seek and save the lost.[9] He came not to condemn those who were sick, but to heal them. Your struggle doesn't place you outside the reach of divine compassion. It places you directly in the line of God's love, mercy, compassion, power, and rescue.

And here is the good news: grace runs toward broken people. Mercy is drawn to wounds. Divine love seeks out the lonely and broken. Redemption doesn't begin when you clean yourself up; it starts the moment you say, *I'm broken, and I need help*. The God who formed galaxies from chaos can create beauty from your ruins.

9. Mark 2:17; Luke 19:10.

So don't shrink back from this naming. Don't hide from the truth of your idolatry or sin. Let the light in. Let the gospel reach where the addiction has ruled. You aren't just a person with a problem. You're a beloved bearer of God's image, caught in a web of false masters. The good news (the gospel) is that the true Master has come to set you free. Father, Son, and Spirit are your Creator, Savior, and Empowerer, so you can trust God to love you, heal you, and set you free.

## Realizing God Sees and Cares

In the hidden hours (those long nights of numbness, regret, or self-contempt), it's easy to believe people and God have forgotten you. Addiction wraps the soul in fog. It torments with the idea that no one sees, no one knows, and no one could care. Shame compounds the silence. You start to believe that your failures have made you invisible. Or worse: unlovable.

But that's a lie with a familiar hiss.

The truth is this: God has seen every moment. Every relapse. Every prayer choked out in the dark. Every tear that fell in secret. The Spirit didn't ignore any of your cries, and didn't overlook any of your shame-filled breaths. You're seen. You're not alone. You're loved and precious to God. The psalmist declares it without hesitation: "The Lord is close to the brokenhearted and saves those who are crushed in spirit" (Ps 34:18). God isn't distant or indifferent, but close.

Scripture offers abundant stories of those who believed their wounds disqualified them.[10] Hagar ran into the desert and found the One who sees. Elijah hid in a cave, and the presence of God found him there. David sinned grievously and still found mercy. The bleeding woman touched the hem of Christ's robe, and he turned to her with tenderness, not disgust. This is the pattern of redemption: God always moves toward the broken, not away from them.

And so, dear fellow pilgrim on the way to freedom and healing, if you imagine God looking at you with crossed arms and a furrowed brow, let that image die. Bury that impression alongside the false gods of condemnation and fear. For the God who seeks you isn't waiting to punish, but to heal. Not watching to tally your stumbles, but to lift you when you fall. Not keeping a record of wrongs, but preparing a robe and a ring.

Think of the prodigal.[11] Think of that long walk home, the speech rehearsed, the shame thick in his throat. And then: a father who runs. Who

10. See Gen 16:13; 1 Kgs 19:9–18; Ps 51; Matt 9:20–22.

11. Luke 15:11–32.

embraces. Who interrupts the apology with celebration. That's the God who sees you now, not as a project to fix but a beloved child to welcome home.

So, take heart. God sees, cares, loves, moves close, and is ready to heal and restore. And the eyes that behold you aren't filled with disappointment, but with compassion strong enough to raise the dead.

## Hope on the Horizon

There's a sacred defiance in hope and a refusal to let despair write the final word. Even after years of relapse, even after bridges burned and promises broken, and even when the future feels like an echo chamber of past mistakes, hope insists: This isn't the end.

And that hope, in Christian recovery, isn't wishful thinking. It's not rooted in your performance, your willpower, or your track record. It's anchored in the resurrection: God's irreversible declaration that death and defeat never get the last say. "If anyone is in Christ," the apostle writes, "the new creation has come: The old has gone, the new is here" (2 Cor 5:17). That isn't a poetic flourish. It's blood-sealed truth.

Around the world, in quiet church basements and busy counseling rooms, in hospital wards and prison cells, stories of recovery are unfolding. Not perfect stories. Not always linear. But real. People who once felt hopeless now walk in freedom. They wake up without craving the thing that used to own them. They pray with clarity. They parent with tenderness. They serve. They forgive. They smile with unburdened hearts. They aren't superhuman: they're proof that God still delivers captives.

You may wonder if such freedom is possible for you. Maybe you've tried before. Perhaps you've fallen more times than you can count. Possibly, shame still weighs heavily on your shoulders. Hear this: God doesn't count you out. Grace doesn't come with an expiration date.[12] Mercy doesn't tire.

In this book, I'm not offering a magic wand. I won't promise a shortcut. Instead, my story (and the stories of countless others throughout history) are witnesses to God's power, freedom, and hope. We testify to the God who specializes in new beginnings. We tell of the horizon of healing that still awaits you. You may not feel it now. But something sacred is already stirring. A quiet dawn just beyond the night.

Hope, healing, and wholeness live. And their name is Jesus Christ.

And through him, new creation isn't only possible; it's already begun.

12. Phil 1:6.

## The Decision to Seek Help

There comes a moment when the heart leans toward freedom. It may come quietly, in the weariness of yet another failure, or with thunder, when everything collapses. But in either case, it's a moment of holy invitation. For me, it came just before the birth of my third daughter, when I realized that my alcoholism might kill me before I had the chance to see her and my other daughters grow up. Did I want to know them and my future grandchildren, or cling to alcohol and never have that chance? To recognize the pain, to feel the loss of what addiction has stolen, and then to say, "I need help," isn't weakness. It's wisdom clothed in humility. It's the first courageous act on the path toward wholeness.

For too long, you may have walked alone, gritting your teeth through relapses, numbing the shame, pretending to have control. But healing was never meant to be a solitary endeavor. The spiritual life (and the recovery life) requires community, honesty, and dependence. This is the paradox of grace: when we admit our need, we become genuinely open to receive abundance.

Now is the time to reach out. Cry out to God, not as a distant deity, but as the One who has been waiting, watching, loving, holding, and longing for your return. This cry doesn't need to be eloquent. A groan, a tear, a desperate "Help me": These are prayers heaven understands. But don't stop there. Seek out a fellow traveler. Call a trusted friend. Find a pastor, sponsor, or recovery group. Addiction isolates, but healing gathers. In these vulnerable spaces of connection, you'll begin to find strength: not just your own, but strength multiplied in shared burdens and mutual encouragement.

The decision to seek help marks a significant turning point. It's not the end of struggle, but the beginning of possibility. God walks with those who move toward light, even if they do so with stumbling and trembling steps. Scripture is filled with those who cried out and were met with mercy. "This poor one called," the psalmist says, "and the Lord heard and saved them out of all their troubles."[13] Let this be your story, too.

Every step forward is honored. Every plea for help is sacred. Don't underestimate the power of one decision. Even the smallest "yes" to healing is met with a warm and heartfelt welcome from God.

Now, having faced the reality of bondage and named the hidden wounds, take a breath. Let this be a holy pause, a moment to sit in the truth that you're not alone, not forgotten, not beyond grace. Even here, in the rawness of recognition, the Spirit speaks to your heart, saying, "You're seen. You're loved. You have a future. And the journey to freedom has already begun."

13. Ps 34:6.

## Reflection Questions

1. What barriers have kept me from admitting I need help (pride, fear, denial, control)?
2. When have I glimpsed the grace of God meeting me in weakness, not strength?
3. What does it stir in me to think that grace is a gift, not something I must earn?
4. How does it feel to admit I can't fix this on my own?
5. What would it mean to truly believe that God delights in walking with me through this?

## Action Steps

1. Make a "grace inventory": List five moments in your life when you felt undeserved kindness or love.
2. Say aloud, once a day, this phrase: "God's grace meets me in my need, not in my perfection."
3. Identify one area where you've been trying to control everything. Practice letting go, prayerfully and practically.
4. Call or meet with someone to simply say, "I think I need help." Let that be a holy beginning.

# 2.

# Faith and Surrender

## Entrusting Your Life to God

For those who've wrestled with addiction, there comes a moment when our soul, weary from striving and spiraling, begins to feel, "There must be more than this." Beneath the wreckage of addiction and the sense of powerlessness, a sacred invitation stirs: the Spirit's call to trust the One who still speaks calm into chaos, breathes new life into the dust, and offerings springs of living water in the desert.[1]

### Believing God Can Restore You

Faith isn't the denial of pain; it's the defiant conviction that pain isn't the end of the story. After admitting powerlessness, a strange question emerges: Can things change? Can something so broken ever be whole again? Faith begins not by answering with certainty, but by daring to believe that God is both able and willing to restore.

Scripture is rich with stories of restoration: bleeding women healed by a single touch, lepers made clean, outcasts welcomed, demons driven out, shame transformed into song, and relationships restored. These aren't ancient myths. They're portraits of what happens when divine love meets human desperation. They show us that God specializes in taking care of the lost causes. No wound is too deep. No history too tangled. No person is too far gone.

1. See Gen 2:7; John 7:37–39; Mark 4:39.

Jesus walked toward those whom everyone else avoided. He reached into the graves of despair and called people back to life. He spoke to the storm inside the soul and said, "Peace, be still." He saw the man chained by demons and restored him to his right mind. These aren't metaphors. They're promises wrapped in flesh.[2]

Believing God can restore you isn't about conjuring emotional certainty. It's about planting a seed of hope in barren soil and trusting that, in time, something holy will grow. You may still feel the cravings. The shame may still linger. The future may still seem foggy. But faith says, "You aren't finished." What was shattered can be mended. What was wasted can be redeemed.

"Nothing is impossible with God," Jesus said; not even your recovery, not even your renewal, and not even your liberation from addiction.[3] This isn't a shallow positivity or naive optimism. It's a deep, rugged, Spirit-empowered belief forged in prayer, Scripture, and the stories of those who've gone before: people who once sat where you sit now and slowly walked into freedom.

So let your next breath carry faith. Let it bring the belief that God isn't only real but present, not only mighty but merciful, and not only able but ready. If you can believe that God can restore even you, then this is already the beginning of your healing, not by your strength, but by the One who raises the dead to life.

## Understanding God's Love and Character

So many begin the journey of recovery haunted by distorted images of God. Some see a cold judge, keeping score from the heavens. Others an angry parent, waiting to punish and scold. Others envision a distant presence, too vast to care for one small, stumbling soul. Others a critical master, unhappy with who they are. Still others carry wounds inflicted in the name of God, wounds that confuse holiness with harshness and discipline with rejection. But to walk this path of healing, the heart must meet the truth of who God really is.

God isn't the shaming voice that echoes after every relapse. God isn't the silence you feared after your last desperate prayer. The sacred texts tell a different story: one of unfailing love, patient mercy, and faithful pursuit. "The Lord is compassionate and gracious," the psalmist declares, "slow to

2. See Luke 8:26–39; Mark 5:25–34; Luke 17:11–19.

3. Luke 1:37.

anger, abounding in love."[4] Not measured love. Not tentative love. Abounding. Overflowing. Uncontainable. God's love is astonishing, extravagant, and poured out for you and me. You can trust that love, depend on that love, and feel safe in that love. Love is at the heart of who God is, for "God is love."[5]

God is the Shepherd who leaves the ninety-nine to find the one wandering in the shadows.[6] God is the Healer who binds up the wounds no one else sees. God is the Parent who scans the horizon, waiting for the child to return: not with punishment in hand, but with open arms and a robe for the weary shoulders.

When we truly see the character of God (holy yet tender, just yet merciful, sovereign yet near), we begin to trust. And trust is what recovery demands. God's Spirit invites you to lay down control, to surrender your defenses, to risk love again. That risk becomes possible not because you're strong, but because God is good and loving.

Even now, as your eyes skim these words, God has been at work. In your longing. In your pain. In your reading. The invitation wasn't random. It's grace that brought you here, and grace will carry you through. God hasn't given up on you. Not now. Not once. Not ever.

The way forward begins not with effort, but with revelation: seeing that the One who calls you to healing is full of compassion, rich in love, and endlessly faithful. Your healing, recovery, and freedom are the overflow of God's character and love, and the Spirit of Christ is here for you now to comfort, restore, liberate, heal, and love you.

## Jesus the Savior and Healer

In the Gospels, Jesus moves with fierce compassion. He doesn't avoid the broken. He seeks them. Touches them. Speaks life into their shame. To follow Jesus isn't to assent to a doctrine; it's to encounter a Person whose very presence brings healing. The same One who calmed storms and cast out demons now speaks peace into the tempest of addiction.

Jesus never treated pain as an inconvenience. He never rushed past desperation. He looked into the eyes of the afflicted and called them beloved. The leper. The blind man. The woman bleeding for twelve years. The possessed, the paralyzed, the forgotten.[7] To each, he brought healing

4. Ps 103:8.
5. 1 John 4:8.
6. Luke 15:3–7.
7. See Mark 1:40–45; John 9:1–12; Mark 5:25–34.

not only of body but of soul. Restoration. Dignity. Freedom. His mission remains unchanged: "To proclaim good news to the poor . . . to bind up the brokenhearted . . . to proclaim liberty to the captives."[8]

This isn't abstract theology. This is practical hope. Recovery through Christ isn't limited to eternity; it begins now. Chains break in real time. Patterns shift. The soul learns how to breathe again. And it happens not through willpower alone, but by a power greater than yourself. The resurrection power that raised Jesus from the dead now works in those who trust in him.[9] This isn't a metaphor. It's a mystery turned reality.

To believe in Jesus is to entrust your broken pieces to the only One who can make them whole. It's to say, "I can't save myself," and to find in return a grace that saves, heals, and sustains. This isn't the cheap grace of sentimentality. It's a grace that meets you where you are but never leaves you there. This is a grace that walks with you through withdrawals, through cravings, through the shame and the rebuilding and the quiet mornings when you wonder if healing will last. This is a grace that can move you from sin, bondage, despair, and death to forgiveness, freedom, hope, and life, just as God raised Christ from death to life, and offered restoration to all humanity and creation.

Jesus didn't come for the righteous but for the sick, the lost, the addicted, the ashamed.[10] This is good news. Because if you're reading this and wondering if you're too far gone, you're exactly the kind of person Jesus came for.

Let this truth sink in: Jesus saves, and Jesus heals. And if you trust him with your whole life (including the parts you'd rather hide), you'll find a power strong enough to set captives free. That includes you.

## What Surrender Really Means

Surrender is often misunderstood. It sounds like waving a white flag in defeat, like losing the war within. But true surrender, the kind that heals and liberates, isn't about defeat; it's about trust. It's not the collapse of identity, but the rediscovery of it in the presence of the One who never stopped calling us by name.

Surrender is like a patient entrusting their life to a gifted surgeon. No one steps onto the operating table and micromanages the scalpel. They lie down, vulnerable and open, consenting to the deep work of healing. There's

8. Isa 61:1.

9. See Rom 8:11.

10. See Mark 2:17; Luke 5:31–32.

courage and faith in vulnerability and surrender that we often underestimate and undervalue. So too, recovery begins when we stop trying to stitch ourselves together with trembling hands and entrust the broken pieces of our lives into divine hands.

To surrender is to hand over not just the addiction, but everything: the secret shame, the fears we've never voiced, the hopes we hardly dare to name. It means saying, "Not my will, but yours be done," and meaning it not just once, but daily.[11] It's to rise each morning and whisper, "Lead me. I don't want to drive anymore."

Surrender isn't a cage. It's the door swung open after years of confinement. Addiction was a cruel master: It demanded more than we could give and repaid us in isolation, torment, and loss. But God is a kind master. Where addiction drained us, God restores. Where it shamed, God dignifies. Where it wounded, God binds up. Surrendering to such a presence isn't bondage. It's freedom.

So, if you've feared the word "surrender," let it be reframed. This isn't resignation, it's resurrection. It's trusting that God's way is better than the one that led you here. It's laying down control and discovering that the One who now leads you has never stopped loving you. This is the holy beginning. This is where hope breathes again.

## Letting Go of Self-Reliance

There's a voice inside many of us that says, "You can fix this. Be strong. Depend on yourself. Grit your teeth. You don't need anyone." It sounds brave. It feels strong. It echoes the self-reliant way of the world. But for the person tangled in addiction, it's a lie dressed in valor, and an unhelpful way to approach freedom from addiction. The truth is, if self-effort could save us, we'd be free already.

White-knuckling change doesn't work. We grit our teeth. We swear this time will be different. We set alarms, make promises, and purge the hidden stash. But time and again, the cravings come, and self-made strength buckles. Because willpower may restrain the hand for a while, but it can't heal the heart. And without heart-change, the cycle repeats.

Scripture tells a story of Peter stepping out of the boat to walk on water. As long as his eyes were fixed on Christ, he stood firm. But the moment he looked at the wind and waves, he began to sink. That story is our story. We've been trying to walk on water alone, and we're drowning. But just as

11. Luke 22:42.

Christ reached out to Peter, God reaches for us, not with condemnation, but with compassion.

Letting go of self-reliance isn't weakness. It's wisdom. Proverbs says, "Trust in the Lord with all your heart and lean not on your understanding."[12] The invitation is clear: Stop trying to navigate this storm with a broken compass. Depend on God instead. Lean into grace, not just grit.

Recovery isn't achieved alone. It's walked hand in hand with God, and shoulder to shoulder with others. We don't need to prove ourselves worthy of healing. We need only to ask for help. So lay down the illusion of control. It hasn't served you well. Let grace carry what your strength can't.

## Overcoming Fear of the Unknown

There's a peculiar terror that arises when the crutch is taken away. What will life look like without the drink, the pill, the screen, the work, the pornography, or the secret habit? Who am I without this coping mechanism? How can I enter this unfamiliar place without my habits? Addiction may be painful, but it's familiar. Freedom, by contrast, can feel like standing at the edge of a vast and uncertain ocean.

Fear says, "What if you fail again? What if it's worse on the other side?" And yet, deeper still, another voice calls, "Come." It's the voice that called Lazarus from the tomb. The voice that called Peter from the boat. The voice that called the people of Israel to leave Egypt for the Promised Land, but first to cross the strange, unfamiliar desert. The voice that says, "Don't be afraid. I'll go with you."

Yes, surrender can be scary. The future is unclear. But here's the truth: we don't need to know what the path holds. We only need to know the One who walks beside us. The Spirit of Christ is with us to comfort, guide, and hold us through change. God never promises a road map, but always promises presence. And that presence is enough.

Jeremiah speaks for the divine heart: "I know the plans I have for you . . . plans to prosper you and not to harm you, plans to give you hope and a future."[13] These aren't words of sentiment. They're declarations of intent. God doesn't lead us from bondage only to abandon us in the wilderness.

So, name your fears. Don't hide from them. Speak them aloud in prayer. And then dare to trust. Dare to believe that the God who knit you together has not abandoned you to this war. The hands that shaped your

12. Prov 3:5.

13. Jer 29:11.

soul know how to rebuild it.[14] Faith isn't the absence of fear. It's choosing to trust even when fear is loud.

Take the next step, even if it's small. Walk into the unknown, not alone, but with the assurance that light always meets those who move toward it. On the far side of this fear is a freedom more spacious than you've ever known.

## The Act of Surrender

Words have power. Especially when they are the honest cry of a broken heart lifted toward God. That's why surrender mustn't stay an abstract idea. It must become an embodied act. The heart must speak. The soul must kneel. The will must yield. And the lips must pray.

You don't need perfect words. Just true ones. Something like, "God, I can't do this. I've tried and failed. I need you. I hand over this addiction, this fear, this pain. Lead me. Please heal me. I surrender to your care." That's a holy prayer. That's the beginning of everything.

Maybe today you mark it down. You write the date in the margin of this book or the corner of your journal. Not because magic happens in a moment, but because milestones matter. You'll look back on this day as the day you stopped running. The day you gave God the keys. The day you stopped fighting alone.

Invite God into every part of your life, not just the addiction. Invite God into the mornings when you wake in shame, the nights when temptation knocks, the relationships that ache, and the places that still feel tender. Invite God to be not just a helper, but your healer, your center, your joy.

And then, follow through. Surrender isn't static. It breathes and moves. It's renewed daily. Each morning becomes a fresh commitment: "God, this day is yours." Each temptation becomes a place of prayer: "God, carry me through this." Each setback becomes an invitation to return: "God, I need you again."

You aren't required to be perfect. You're only asked to be honest and willing. The journey of recovery is long, but it's paved with grace. And you don't walk it alone. The One who holds all things together now holds you. So, say the prayer. Commit. Write the date. And take the next step forward in the company of mercy.

14. Ps 139:13–14.

## Embracing God's Will Daily

In our modern age, we're tempted to think that change should happen quickly, perhaps even instantaneously. But that's rarely the way. Change is often a slow and arduous process, and in the spiritual life, it requires surrender to God. Humans tend to resist surrendering their will, desires, and control, which slows recovery and change down even further. Surrender isn't a single moment carved in the past; it's a rhythm for the present. It's not a monument we build once and walk away from. It's like a well we draw from daily. A humble prayer before our feet hit the floor: "God, I surrender this day to you. I can't do this in my power. Please guide me. Strengthen me. Keep me sober. Be near."

Each day brings its temptations, its small decisions that shape the course of our becoming. Addiction thrives in chaos, secrecy, and self-will. But surrender breathes in rhythm, simplicity, honesty, transparency, and trust. The work of recovery (real, sustained, spiritual, Spirit-empowered recovery) happens not in grand gestures but in humble acts of alignment: choosing a walk instead of a binge, calling a sponsor instead of isolating, telling the truth instead of lies, turning to Scripture instead of spiraling in shame. These small acts of trust and intention accumulate to create healing.

God's will isn't some cryptic puzzle we must anxiously decode. It's revealed in the loving prompts of the Spirit, the wise guidance of Scripture, the counsel of wise companions, the conviction of conscience, and the Spirit's nudge toward life and truth. When we pause, pray, and pay attention, we begin to recognize the pattern of divine love unfolding in our choices.

And what's God's will? Not control. Not punishment. Not perfection. God's will is that we be made whole. That we live with clarity and courage. That we recover not just sobriety, but a life of purpose, peace, and love. That our faith in Christ's work sustains us, our hope in God's redemption and healing transforms us, and our love for God and our neighbors shows that we've become disciples of Jesus Christ. This is the will of One who delights in our freedom more than we do.

Recovery demands more than detox. It calls for reordering. And in the daily surrender to God's will, we find that new order rising from the rubble. Slowly, a sacred structure replaces the chaos: mornings anchored in prayer, friendships grounded in truth, habits shaped around discipleship and spiritual formation, and time spent not numbing but creating, serving, resting, and connecting. This is how healing deepens; not overnight, but one surrendered decision at a time.

Over weeks and months, the fruit begins to show. The fog lifts. Relationships start to mend. Courage returns. Purpose flickers to life again. This isn't because we tried harder, but because we aligned our lives with the One whose will leads us into abundant life.

So today, before you reach for anything else, reach for God. Say the prayer. Listen for the next right step. Align again. And know this: the daily surrender of your will isn't weakness, it's wisdom. It's not failure, it's formation. And it's not the end, it's the way forward.

## Trust and Obey

Faith isn't a warm feeling, a soft sentimentality, or a vague belief. Faith is a courageous decision, a brave letting go of control, and a lived surrender. Trust that doesn't move is just sentiment. But trust that walks, acts, and obeys—that's where the power is, and that's where recovery begins to take flesh.

It's not enough to say, "I trust God." Trust is revealed when we do what trust requires. When we walk into the recovery meeting, even though we're terrified. When we empty the stash and delete the contacts. When we forgive the one who wounded us or call the one we wounded. When we change our schedule, delete the app, avoid the pub, cancel the subscription, or break off the toxic relationship. These aren't just behavioral adjustments. They're acts of obedience. They're spiritual revolutions in ordinary clothes.

The Letter of James puts it plainly: "Faith without works is dead."[15] James doesn't mean that our works earn grace (they don't); he means that genuine faith bears fruit. Obedience isn't the condition of God's love; it's the response to it. When we believe that God is who God says, and will do what God has promised, our lives begin to align. We act. We step. We change. We trust. We obey. Not to earn healing, but to inhabit it.

Each act of obedience strengthens the foundation. Like bricks laid one by one, small steps of faith slowly build a life worth living. At first, it may feel awkward, unnatural, and even terrifying. But over time, new habits form. Courage grows. The path becomes clearer. And our actions begin to reflect the transformation happening within.

Obedience also reconnects us to joy. Not the fleeting thrill of escape that addiction offers, but the deep, soul-settling joy that comes from living in harmony with God. Such joy is supernatural, offered by Jesus Christ and made possible in the power of his Spirit. Each step of obedience is a yes to life, a yes to freedom, and a yes to God's healing.

And here's the grace: When we stumble (and we will), God doesn't reject us. The path doesn't vanish. The invitation still stands. This truth has been a saving grace to me so many times, when I've stumbled or slipped

15. Jas 2:17.

back into addiction. But the good news is that we don't need to be flawless to keep walking forward. We need only be willing.

So, take the next step. Ask, "What's one concrete act of trust I can take today?" Then do it. Trust is proven in action. And every act of obedience is a seed of resurrection. Water it with courage, tend it with prayer, and watch what God can do.

## A New Master, A New Freedom

Addiction is a master that disguises itself as relief. It offers comfort, escape, and release, but only for a moment. Then it tightens its grip. What once felt like freedom soon reveals itself as a form of slavery. Addiction demands more and more while giving less and less. It makes promises it can't keep and exacts a cost greater than you ever meant to pay. You don't use it; it uses you.

In that bondage, the soul forgets its name. The heart shrinks. Joy withers. Purpose leaks away. And shame, that cruel companion, whispers that this is all you'll ever know. You begin to think of yourself not as a person with addiction, but as the addiction itself: defined by it, doomed to it.

But in surrender, a shift begins. You step out from under the tyranny of addiction and into the arms of a new Master: not one who condemns but who calls you beloved, and not one who enslaves but who liberates. Christ doesn't demand everything and return only silence. Christ gives everything and asks only your trust.

Jesus's invitation is tender but radical: "Come to me . . . and I'll give you rest."[16] Not exhaustion. Not shame. Not another impossible standard. Rest. Recovery begins with the realization that rest is holy. That freedom isn't self-made but gifted. That healing doesn't begin with performance, but with presence.

Serving Christ isn't trading one prison for another. It's waking up in your right mind. It's laying down the weapons you've used against yourself. It's learning to walk again, this time in love, with dignity, on solid ground. Addiction promised relief but delivered ruin. Christ promises rest and delivers resurrection.

In this new relationship, obedience becomes joy. Discipline becomes delight. You begin to see that surrender was not defeat, but deliverance. You're not just saying no to addiction, you're saying yes to life, to hope, to becoming more fully human, more fully loved, more fully free.

16. Matt 11:28.

So don't fear the language of mastery. The question was never, "Will I serve something?" It was always, "What will I serve?"[17] Addiction is a cruel master. Christ is a kind one. And under Christ's care, the wilderness becomes a garden again.

You haven't traded one bondage for another. You've come home. You've found the One who doesn't exploit your weakness but redeems it. This is the freedom you were created for: not the absence of all limits, but the presence of perfect love.

Take a breath here, and let it settle into your soul: the One you're surrendering to isn't a tyrant, but a healer, a companion, a redeemer whose love restores what addiction tried to steal. This is holy ground, where powerlessness becomes possibility, and trust becomes the doorway to a new way of living.

## Reflection Questions

1. What do I most struggle to surrender (my image, habits, pain, past, control)?
2. How has my definition of faith changed over time? Is it more about trust than certainty?
3. What fears surface when I think about surrendering my whole life to God?
4. Where have I seen God prove trustworthy, even in difficulty?
5. What would it look like to entrust every part of my story to divine grace?

## Action Steps

1. Choose one tangible thing to surrender this week (a routine, a toxic habit, a secret). Offer it to God daily in prayer.
2. Begin your morning with this breath prayer: "Into your hands, I commit this day."
3. Journal each evening: "Where did I try to control today? Where did I trust instead?"
4. Pray the prayer of surrender from the chapter aloud each day, slowly and intentionally.

17. Matt 6:24.

# 3.

# Renewing the Mind

## Replacing Lies with God's Truth

Some battles are fought in the flesh, but the fiercest ones are waged in the mind. Long after the substance is gone, the presence of addiction still whispers lies. Yet, it's here that transformation begins: when the soul dares to believe a new story, and truth begins to rewrite the script of the heart and mind.

### The Battlefield of the Mind

Recovery begins in the soul, but it's waged in the mind. The terrain is internal, yet the consequences spill out into every corner of life. Thoughts, like seeds, root themselves in our inner soil. Some grow into hope and clarity. Others choke us with despair and distortion.

Addiction rewires the brain. It offers lies until they sound like the truth. "You're too far gone." "You always mess this up." "One more time won't matter." "God's not really interested in you." These thoughts become the script we live by, even when we know better. And over time, the script becomes a stronghold.

But Scripture calls us to a holy revolt: "Take every thought captive to make it obedient to Christ."[1] That's not a gentle metaphor; it's a battle cry. There are patterns of thought that must be confronted, dismantled, and

1. 2 Cor 10:5.

replaced with truth. Not just positive thinking, but transformed thinking. A mind renewed by the Spirit's a mind made free.

You aren't your thoughts. But you're responsible for them. What you let play in the background of your mind will eventually shape your emotions, choices, and identity. This is why vigilance is vital. Not anxious perfectionism, but alertness: watching what thoughts creep in, what stories you tell yourself, what voices you allow to take up residence.

The spiritual life isn't abstract. It's concrete. It meets you at 7 a.m. when your first thought is self-loathing. It meets you in the car when a wave of craving or regret hits. It meets you in moments of silence when old scripts start replaying. And in those very moments, you're not alone.

The Spirit's present, offering another way. Scripture is a prophetic yet healing balm, not a slogan. The Bible, which is the "sword of the Spirit," cuts through illusion.[2] Prayer reorients our souls. Community is a spiritual reinforcement. In these, the lies begin to lose their power.

What if your next act of faith isn't a grand gesture, but simply refusing to believe the lie that says, "You'll never change"? What if victory looks like interrupting the cycle with one true word: "No more. I belong to God now."

This battle isn't won overnight. But it can be won. Slowly, steadily, one surrendered thought at a time. And as you learn to guard your mind, you reclaim your life. What once felt automatic becomes interruptible. What once enslaved you becomes exposed. And in that exposure, grace floods in.

You aren't powerless here. You have a Defender. You have the mind of Christ.[3] And that means you have a future not dictated by fear, but shaped by love.

## Identifying the Lies You Believe

Every addiction is tethered to a lie.[4] Sometimes the lie whispers. Sometimes it shouts. But it always hides in the shadows, shaping behavior long before it's named. These lies aren't abstract; they're profoundly personal, buried beneath trauma, shame, unmet need, and distorted identity. Recovery isn't merely about abstaining from a substance or a behavior. It's about confronting and uprooting the lies that made the addiction feel necessary in the first place.

Many carry lies about themselves: "I'm unlovable." "I'll never be enough." "I'm too far gone." Others have absorbed corrosive beliefs about

2. Eph 6:17.

3. 1 Cor 2:16.

4. May, *Addiction and Grace*, 34–36.

the world: "No one really cares." "Everyone leaves." "People only want something from me." And still others have swallowed lies about God: "God's angry with me." "God has abandoned me." "God might help others, but not someone like me."

These lies often take root early. A child abandoned by a parent may grow up believing, "I'm not worth staying for." A teen bullied or overlooked may start to think, "I'm invisible and unwanted." An adult spiraling in secret addiction may interpret every failure as evidence that they're beyond redemption. And when those lies remain unchallenged, they become the lens through which life is lived and addiction is justified.

Consider the story of Daniel, a man I once knew, who relapsed after three years of sobriety.[5] When he traced it back, the trigger wasn't just stress or isolation. It was a moment when he felt unworthy of love. He hadn't named that belief before, but it was always there, lurking beneath the surface: "I'm only lovable when I'm performing perfectly." When he failed, the old voice returned, and the lie opened the door to escape through substance again.

Naming these lies isn't easy. They often masquerade as truth because they've been rehearsed for years. But recovery demands light. And the moment you name a lie, you begin to rob it of its power. This practice of reflection and pausing to ask, "What am I believing right now that may not be true?," isn't a one-time task. It's daily spiritual discernment. It's a confession. It's unlearning.

And hear this: You aren't alone in this work. Everyone in recovery walks this road. Every soul being healed by grace has had to dismantle false narratives and confront internal strongholds. Naming the lies isn't a sign of failure; it's a sign that freedom is beginning.

## Embracing God's Truth About You

If lies fuel addiction, then recovery is rooted in truth. Not vague optimism. Not empty affirmations. But truth: unshakable, Spirit-breathed, Scripture-rooted truth about who you are and who God is. To walk in freedom, you must begin to see yourself not through the shattered lens of addiction, but through the tender eyes of the One who made you, knows you, and has never stopped loving you.

Start with this: You're loved. Not because of your performance. Not because of your sobriety streak. Not because you've finally "cleaned up." You're loved because God is love, and love isn't earned; it's received. "God demonstrates divine love for us in this: while we were still sinners, Christ

5. I've changed his name for privacy and confidentiality reasons.

died for us."[6] That means before you even considered change, before you knew how lost you were, love had already come looking for you.

If you've believed the lie, "I'm unforgivable," hear this: "As far as the east is from the west, so far has God removed your transgressions from you."[7] If the lie says, "I'll never change," cling to this truth: "I can do all things through Christ who gives me strength."[8] If shame tells you, "I'm too broken to be used," remember: "We have this treasure in jars of clay, to show that this all-surpassing power is from God and not from us."[9]

These aren't just memory verses. They're spiritual weapons. They're light piercing the darkness. They're seeds that, when planted in the soil of belief, grow into hope and identity and strength.

Here's a practice to begin: Write down the lie you tend to believe. Then find one verse (just one) that tells a different story. Keep it close. Read it aloud. Memorize it. Let it interrupt the old script. When the old voice rises, saying, "You'll fail again," "You're disgusting," "You're alone," speak the truth back to it: "God delights in me," "I'm fearfully and wonderfully made,"[10] "Nothing can separate me from the love of God."[11]

As you do this, your mind begins to be renewed. Slowly, the grooves of addiction's story are overwritten by the narrative of grace. Slowly, your self-perception shifts from shame to sonship, from victimhood to belovedness. Slowly, the truth becomes not just something you recite but something you believe.

This isn't magic. It's formation. It's spiritual warfare. It's healing at the level of identity. And it'll change everything.

## The Practice of Mind Renewal

The mind is the soil where freedom or captivity first takes root. What we ponder, rehearse, absorb, and believe slowly shapes the contours of our character and the choices we make. Romans 12:2 doesn't ask for mere surface adjustment; it calls for metamorphosis: "Be transformed by the renewing of your mind." The apostle Paul exhorts disciples to stop conforming to the ways and thinking of the world and instead to detox the soul from distorted narratives and beliefs, bathing the interior life in God's divine,

6. Rom 5:8.
7. Ps 103:12.
8. Phil 4:13.
9. 2 Cor 4:7.
10. Ps 139:14.
11. Rom 8:38–39.

eternal truth, and pursuing transformation by renewing our minds. Instead of allowing our minds to dwell on lies, we choose to meditate on the Bible and discern God's "good, pleasing and perfect will."[12]

This renewal isn't a one-time event. It's daily work: a sacred rhythm of cleaning out the mind's debris and replacing it with wisdom that restores. For those in recovery, the mind is often haunted by lies and habituated responses. It's like a vessel once filled with poison; you don't just empty it once. You rinse it repeatedly with the pure water of Scripture, grace, and contemplative truth, until new clarity and life emerge.[13] During my first year of recovery, I immersed myself in the Bible, asking the Holy Spirit to reshape my thinking and lifestyle, filling me with the power, conviction, and grace I needed.

Begin each day by reading even a small portion of Scripture. Don't read the Bible to check a box but to tune your inner life to a deeper frequency. Linger on a phrase. Let it echo into the places where fear or shame once lived. Supplement this with journaling, not to record the day but to interrupt distorted thinking. Write down the lies you're tempted to believe ("I'll never change," "I'm alone," "I'm too far gone," etc.), and then, beside them, write truths that disrupt those lies with grace and power. The goal isn't perfection but pattern. With consistency, thought pathways begin to shift. Emotional reactions become less impulsive. Temptations lose their grip.

Mind renewal also means being mindful of what you take in. What are you listening to on the commute? What messages are reinforced in your playlists, conversations, and social media feed? Choose what nourishes your spirit: faith-filled podcasts, worship music, and contemplative silence. Let truth be louder than the noise.

As the old patterns are gently uprooted and replaced by holy habits, desires begin to align with the Spirit. What once felt irresistible begins to lose power. You may not notice it immediately, but months down the road, you'll realize you're reacting with peace instead of panic, gratitude instead of shame, love instead of self-loathing, faith instead of cynicism, and hope instead of despair. This is the slow, radiant fruit of a mind transformed not by willpower, but by grace woven into practice.

## The Bible as a Weapon and Resource Against Temptation

Temptation doesn't merely knock. Temptation lurks, prods, schemes, and waits for moments of weariness. We all face temptation and need to

12. Rom 12:2.

13. May, *Addiction and Grace*, 139.

consider how to respond beforehand. In the wilderness, even Jesus faced temptation, but he didn't fight it with clever arguments or sheer will. He wielded Scripture like a sword, not as a blunt weapon of shame but as a precise, trusted tool to cut through temptation and deceit. "It is written," he said, repeatedly, naming truth in the face of lies.[14]

Those walking the road of recovery must do the same. The cravings will come. So will the voices (internal and external) that say, "Just once more," or "You haven't changed," or "No one sees." In these moments, Scripture becomes not just a comfort, but a counterstrike, a shield, a staff, and a light on a darkened path. When you feel too weak to resist, declare aloud, "God's grace is sufficient for me, for power is made perfect in weakness" (2 Cor 12:9). When shame resurfaces, say, "There is now no condemnation for those who are in Christ Jesus" (Rom 8:1). When you feel isolated, speak, "Never will I leave you; never will I forsake you" (Heb 13:5).

Write these verses down. Carry them in your pocket or your phone. Place them where you'll see them: on a mirror, a dashboard, the inside cover of your journal. Recite them when temptation tightens its grip. Let them become your reflex, your anchor, your way of declaring war on the old lies with divine ammunition.

This isn't magic; it's formation. Over time, you're training your mind to recognize deceit and choose truth. The Scripture doesn't erase the struggle, but it reframes it. It reminds you of who you are and whose you are. It pulls you out of isolation and reminds you that the Spirit who raised Christ from the dead lives in you, empowering your freedom.[15]

Temptation loses its power not simply when you say "no," but when you say "yes" to something greater: yes to life, yes to truth, yes to freedom, yes to love, and yes to God. And Scripture is the language of that "yes." It invites you to speak back to the darkness with light. It steadies you. It says, "You aren't alone." It reminds you that though temptation is real, grace is stronger, and the way of escape is always near.

## Prayer and Taking Thoughts Captive

The mind is a battleground, and thoughts often arrive like uninvited guests, some leading to joy and peace, others wielding knives. For those in recovery, the mind can become a theater of torment, replaying old lies, projecting future failures, tempting with images, memories, or imagined relief. But the sacred gift of prayer reclaims that space. It's not performance or ritual;

14. Matt 4:1–11; Eph 6:17.

15. Rom 8:11.

it's relationship. It's the soul's breath, rising in the moment when craving strikes or despair tightens its grip. Prayer offers us the chance to depend on a power and love beyond ourselves, knowing that when we're weak or tempted, God's empowering presence helps us in our need.[16]

Prayer can be as raw and straightforward as: "God, I need help right now. Take this craving from me. Fill my mind with your peace instead." It's in that honest turning that the Spirit meets us. Philippians 4:6–7 offers more than comfort; it offers a battle plan: "Do not be anxious about anything, but in every situation, by prayer and petition, with thanksgiving, present your requests to God." The result? "The peace of God, which transcends all understanding, will guard your hearts and minds in Christ Jesus." Prayer becomes both shield and balm. It guards. It steadies. It replaces the gnawing ache with holy presence. It reminds us of God's unconditional, extravagant love for us, regardless of how our lives have turned out or how we may feel about ourselves or what others may say about us. Prayer offers a chance to sit at Jesus's feet and hear him call us "beloved."

But prayer also works in tandem with vigilance. The apostle Paul instructs us to take every thought captive and make it obedient to Christ (2 Cor 10:5). Not every thought deserves to reside in our minds. Not every feeling is prophecy. The lie that says, "I'll always be an addict," or "I need this to cope," must be interrogated, not coddled. We don't need to believe everything we think.

This takes practice. You learn to pause when a thought arises. You name it: "This is shame." You challenge it: "Is this God's voice or my fear?" You replace it: "I'm loved, I'm not alone, I'm being renewed." Pairing this with prayer transforms a reaction into a response. You don't just survive temptation; you transform it into a connection with God. With time, this habit reshapes not only your behavior but your inner landscape. Where once there were thought patterns carved by addiction, now there are pathways carved by grace.

The mind isn't a passive recipient. We can join with God as God forms, sanctifies, and trains our minds toward joy, peace, and freedom. Prayer, coupled with truth, becomes the daily liturgy that leads our souls toward lasting freedom.

16. Alcoholics Anonymous, *Alcoholics Anonymous*, especially step 2 and step 3.

## Dealing with Triggers and Cravings

Cravings aren't only physical; they're environmental, emotional, psychological, and spiritual.[17] They're the echo of past habits calling from the shadows. Cravings strike with little warning: a particular song, a scent, a street, a memory, a stressor. Recovery isn't about eliminating all triggers; it's about recognizing them, acknowledging them, and navigating them with wisdom and grace.

External triggers can be disarmed with intentional action. If a specific bar on the drive home awakens longing, change the route. If scrolling late at night opens the door to relapse, consider turning your phone off by 8 p.m. For me, watching movies late at night was often accompanied by drinking wine, so I needed to stop that practice. These changes to habits or lifestyle aren't acts of avoidance; they're acts of resistance: holy, intentional, prophetic resistance. You aren't running from weakness; you're running toward life.

But not all triggers are external. Many of them hide within, such as boredom, shame, regret, loneliness, or anxiety. You feel the wave rising long before you recognize its name. That's why self-awareness is crucial. Keep a journal or note where your temptations tend to arise. Track the emotional texture of your day. Did you feel unappreciated at work? Did a conversation leave you raw? Did a setting remind you of past pain? Often, the craving that follows isn't about the substance or behavior itself; it's a distorted cry for comfort, connection, or control.

This is where the power of plan and prayer intersect. Have a list of healthy responses: take a walk, call a sponsor, read a psalm, do breath work, go to the gym, listen to praise and worship music, ring a friend, splash cold water on your face. These actions may seem small, but they create a margin between the urge and the action.[18] That margin is where God often meets us.

And don't forget to pray when the trigger hits. Even something short and desperate is enough: "Help me, God. Meet me in this." You don't need to be eloquent; you need to be real. In that moment, you aren't alone. The Spirit groans with you. Christ intercedes for you. The Creator runs toward you.

Over time, the power of triggers diminishes. Not because they vanish, but because your responses become more rooted. The same bar on the corner becomes a landmark of deliverance. The same emotion that once drove you to escape becomes an invitation to prayer. This is the slow, glorious reformation of the soul: learning that you aren't a slave to every feeling

17. Maté, *In the Realm of Hungry Ghosts.*

18. Bowen et al., *Mindfulness-Based Relapse Prevention.*

and you aren't destined to spiral. You're a beloved child of God, and even in the fire of craving, the Spirit and word of Jesus Christ are making you new.

## Cultivating a Healthy Thought Life

Recovery isn't just about subtraction (removing what poisons) but about addition: pouring in what nourishes, heals, and enlivens. It's not enough to cast out the lies; the heart and mind must be filled with what's true and beautiful. The apostle's exhortation in Phil 4:8 serves as a sacred compass for this very journey: "Whatever is true, whatever is noble, whatever is right, whatever is pure, whatever is lovely, whatever is admirable—if anything is excellent or praiseworthy—think about such things."

This isn't a call to escapist positivity or naïve denial of pain. It's an invitation to intentionally shape the interior world with what's worthy of awe and praise. In the shadowlands of addiction, the mind was a storm of accusations, cravings, and confusion. But now, the invitation is to become a curator of the soul: selecting what enters, what stays, what echoes.

One way to begin is through daily gratitude. Keep a list. Write down three things each day you're thankful for, no matter how small. A warm meal. A friend's text. The courage to say no. Gratitude reframes your reality, awakening the soul to abundance where it once saw only lack.[19] It softens the heart, disrupts the spiral of self-pity, and opens space for joy.

Read books that stir the soul. Listen to music that brings peace. Watch the sun rise or set and let it teach you something about beginnings and endings. When your mind starts to wander toward old obsessions or toxic loops, redirect it toward wonder. Ask: What beauty is present here? What truth can I rehearse? What goodness can I dwell on?

The life of the mind isn't sterile or static. It's a garden. Left untended, weeds will take over. But when you plant intentionally (truth, awareness, beauty, prayer, kindness, compassion, love, wisdom), you begin to harvest peace. This isn't about perfection; it's about transformation. The goal isn't to have no bad thoughts but to have minds so full of God's goodness that the lies have less room to breathe.

You aren't just escaping something destructive: you're entering something sacred. Recovery isn't merely the absence from addiction; it's the presence with life. Let the renewing of your mind be a joyful labor. Let every good and noble thought be a stone in the cathedral God is building in you.

19. Emmons, *Thanks!*, 23–24.

## Progress, Not Perfection

In recovery, the lie of perfection is often as dangerous as the addiction itself.[20] It says, "You should be further along by now." It shames you for stumbling. It portrays holiness as an unattainable summit rather than a gradual pilgrimage of grace. But the truth is more straightforward, kinder, and more enduring: this journey is about progress, not perfection.

The renewing of the mind doesn't happen in a single spiritual breakthrough or after one victorious month. It happens inch by inch, day by day, sometimes even moment by moment. Some days you'll feel like a saint, full of clarity and peace. Other days, the old ghosts will come knocking (resentment, lust, despair, self-hatred) and you'll forget everything you thought you'd learned. That's not failure. That's formation.

God isn't tallying your slips like a harsh accountant. God is watching the long arc of your becoming. When the negative thoughts slip in, when you feel tempted to rehearse old patterns, pause: not in shame, but in reflection. Look back. Have your relapses become shorter? Are you catching yourself more quickly? Are you reaching out for help rather than hiding in silence? These are signs of grace at work.

Celebrate the small victories. The day you chose prayer instead of numbing. The moment you walked away from a trigger. The hour you sat with your pain and didn't escape. These are sacred wins. They are the fruit of Spirit-led transformation, however quiet and unseen.

It helps to journal your journey. Not every detail, but the themes, the shifts, the little breakthroughs. It reminds you that healing is real, even when it's slow. When you see how far you've come, your failures lose their sting. They become teachers instead of tyrants.

And when shame tempts you to give up, remember that sanctification is God's work, not yours alone. You participate, but you don't manufacture the change. You surrender, cooperate, and trust, but God is the one reshaping your mind like clay in divine hands. Progress in God's economy isn't linear. It's holy, mysterious, messy, and beautiful.

So, breathe. Keep walking. Don't despise the days of small beginnings.[21] Perfection isn't the goal: faithfulness is. You're not being measured. You're being loved into newness.

20. Alcoholics Anonymous. *Alcoholics Anonymous*, 60.

21. Zech 4:10.

## A New Perspective on Life

When the mind is renewed, the heart begins to breathe differently. Thought patterns shift, and what once felt like a permanent fog begins to clear. Slowly, almost imperceptibly at first, the addict begins to see the world with fresh eyes. This isn't optimism. It's resurrection. What used to entice now repels. What once seemed dull and lifeless (like a quiet morning, a walk in the sun, a simple prayer) now pulses with meaning. The pleasures of old habits are revealed for what they are: hollow whispers promising peace but delivering pain.

Renewal doesn't come all at once. It's more like the dawning of morning: gradual, steady, quiet. There are still shadows. There are still days when the old voice seduces. But the voice of truth grows louder. Peace, not chaos, begins to anchor the soul. The anxious mind discovers rest not because every storm has stilled, but because something deeper has taken root: a holy clarity, a stillness at the center. God's Spirit is retraining the imagination, not just the behavior.

In this new light, even the past looks different. Regret gives way to gratitude: for survival, for grace, for the chance to begin again. What once was shame becomes testimony. And what was hidden in darkness becomes a witness to the healing power of divine mercy.

As desires change, so too does the horizon of possibility. Dreams once discarded begin to stir. Purpose awakens. Compassion deepens. With every step in recovery, the renewed mind doesn't just avoid the old ways; it starts walking in new ones. This is the mind of Christ taking shape within the soul.[22] And this transformation isn't a bonus to recovery; it's the fruit of it.

Hold fast to this hope: that every time you choose truth over lies, light over shadow, presence over escape, you are becoming someone new. You aren't merely avoiding relapse; you are reclaiming the life addiction tried to steal. And in this, the God who renews all things is glorified.

Pause here, breathe deep, and give thanks that the mind once chained can now be transformed, one sacred thought at a time.

## Reflection Questions

1. What negative thoughts or lies have I believed about myself, others, or God? Where might those have originated? Begin with compassionate curiosity. Naming these thoughts without shame allows you to begin replacing them with truth.

22. Cor 2:16; Phil 2:5.

2. Which Scriptures speak most directly to my current mental and spiritual battles? Let the word become personal—allow it to shine a light on dark corners and declare truth over your struggles.
3. How have I already seen my mindset shifting as I engage in prayer, Scripture, or recovery practices? Recognizing even small transformations helps cultivate gratitude and perseverance.
4. When cravings or temptations arise, what responses have helped me most: prayer, truth statements, calling someone, or something else? Noticing what works helps build a personalized spiritual strategy for the mind.
5. What does it look like for me to live with a renewed mind today? In my thoughts, desires, and decisions? This question helps bridge inner transformation with practical daily living.

## Action Steps

1. Write down two or three lies you've believed and next to each one, write a Scripture that tells a better truth. Keep this list in your Bible, journal, or phone. Review it often, especially during moments of temptation or shame.
2. Create a simple morning or evening "mind renewal" routine. It might include reading a psalm, praying through Phil 4:6–8, or listening to a worship song that lifts your perspective.
3. Identify one recurring trigger and plan a spiritual response. For example, if loneliness is a trigger, set a reminder to pray or call a trusted friend. If anxiety overwhelms, repeat a Scripture out loud.
4. Choose one positive thought or truth to meditate on today. Carry it with you, speak it over yourself, and invite God to write it deep into your heart.

# 4.

# Inner Healing

## Confession, Repentance, and Cleansing

Before healing can flood the soul, the doors must be opened wide. We begin this chapter by stepping into a sacred space, where honesty meets grace, where secrets lose their power, and where the slow and holy work of inner cleansing begins. In this sanctuary of confession and repentance, we don't find shame but an invitation to be made whole.

### Bringing Secrets into the Light

Addiction isn't merely a compulsion of the body or a craving of the mind; it's a keeper of secrets. In its grip, we learn to hide: to lie, to compartmentalize, to conceal our shame in shadows. We fear exposure. We dread judgment. We convince ourselves that silence is safer. But what festers in the dark slowly rots the soul.

The gospel invites us into a different reality: one where truth sets us free. "Everything hidden will be revealed," Jesus said, not as a threat but as a promise of liberation.[1] Healing begins the moment light touches what we've kept buried. Shame loses its grip when we dare to say, "This is who I've been. But I don't want to stay here."

The process is terrifying. Naming the truth (whether it's a relapse, a betrayal, a stash hidden in the back of a drawer) can feel like standing naked before the world. But grace always meets honesty. And where there

1. Luke 8:17.

is honesty, there is the Spirit, moving gently but surely to heal what's been fractured.

Confession isn't weakness; it's sacred strength. It breaks the cycle of isolation. It disarms the voice that says, "You'll always be this way." It opens the heart to receive not condemnation, but compassion. And it invites others into our story (trusted friends, mentors, counselors) so that we no longer walk alone.

The enemy thrives on secrecy.[2] But God walks where truth is spoken. So, speak it. Start with God. Say it aloud in prayer. Then consider telling someone you trust. Let the darkness lose its power. Let the chains fall one by one.

This isn't about public shame. It's about private liberation. Some confessions are quiet and sacred, meant only for a trusted guide or a healing circle. But all confession is holy. Because it says, "I believe God's love is bigger than this secret." And in that belief, a new kind of freedom is born.

## Confession to God and Receiving Forgiveness

There's sacred humility in the act of confession: a holy surrender characterized by vulnerability, trust, and dependence on God. In the space where our hearts meet truth, something begins to unravel: the tangled web of shame, secrecy, and self-justification. Confession isn't about groveling before a wrathful deity. It's about stepping into the light, where mercy has already been waiting, hands outstretched, to receive love unconditionally and abundantly.

Scripture offers a promise that pierces through despair like dawn through shadow: "If we confess our sins, God is faithful and just and will forgive us our sins and purify us from all unrighteousness" (1 John 1:9). Notice what it doesn't say. It doesn't say "if we earn forgiveness," or "if we feel bad enough." It says if we confess: if we name the truth, admit the harm, and come with nothing but our need. God responds not with condemnation but with cleansing. Divine justice and mercy meet in that moment, and grace floods in like healing rain.

To confess is to agree with God about what's broken. It's to whisper (or sob, or shout), "Yes, this is what I've done. Yes, it has hurt others and me. Yes, I need healing." But more than that, it's to risk believing the gospel: that forgiveness isn't a theoretical concept but a lived reality, that the blood of Christ is sufficient, and that grace is greater than guilt.

2. Foster, *Celebration of Discipline*, 145–47.

So, what does confession look like in practice? Begin by setting aside the masks. Get still. Let the Spirit search your heart. You don't need poetic language or perfect words, just honesty. Speak plainly: "God, I've been hiding this. I've justified it. I feel guilt and shame." Linger in the truth, but don't stay in the shame. Move forward into the second half of that promise: forgiveness and purification. Not potential, partial, or probational forgiveness and cleansing: immediate, complete, and eternal.

This moment of confession isn't the end; it's a doorway. On the other side lies the beginning of healing. It may take time to feel forgiven, but God's promise is based not on your emotions but on divine faithfulness. Keep coming back to that truth. Memorize it. Recite it when the Accuser whispers lies. And remember: every time you confess, heaven leans in, and grace rushes to meet you.

## Repentance and Changing Direction

Confession cracks open the hardened earth, but repentance is what allows new life to grow. Repentance is the complete turning away from something and toward God and God's forgiveness, healing, and restoration. Repentance is a turning not just of lips but of limbs, not just of thought but of trajectory, and not just of ideas but of habits, disciplines, and practices. In a culture that often equates saying "sorry" with sufficient change, the gospel asks something more profound, more daring: turn around and walk in a different direction.[3]

Repentance means leaving behind the patterns that enslaved you, even when they felt familiar, even when they masqueraded as comfort. It means disrupting the rituals of your addiction: not only the substances or behaviors, but the mental scripts and emotional habits that accompanied them. Repentance is spiritual rebellion against the old self, and it's holy allegiance to a new way of being.

The Hebrew word for repentance, *teshuvah*, literally means "return." Returning means not merely to stop doing wrong, but to return to the One who made you, to the path you were always meant to walk. Likewise, the Greek *metanoia* points to a profound transformation of the mind and heart.[4] Repentance is both an action and an inner reorientation. It's not penance. It's permission to step out of darkness and into light.

Picture this: You are walking west, into the fading shadows, when suddenly you realize the road ends in ruin. To repent isn't to mourn the

3. Volf, *Free of Charge*, 150–53.

4. Kittel and Friedrich, *Theological Dictionary of the New Testament*, s.v. "metanoeō."

distance already walked, it's to turn and begin walking east, toward the rising sun. You don't need to have the whole journey figured out. You only need to take the next step.

Tangible acts of repentance may include deleting contacts that lead you astray, changing daily routines, making amends, installing safeguards, or replacing triggers with life-giving rhythms. It may mean stepping into uncomfortable vulnerability, seeking community, or laying down the pride that says, "I've got this." Repentance isn't about self-perfection; it's about God-dependence. You'll stumble: everyone does. But what matters is the direction of your feet, not the speed of your stride.

As Jesus said, "Produce fruit in keeping with repentance" (Matt 3:8). That fruit might look like integrity where deception once lived, tenderness where cynicism ruled, or discipline where chaos reigned. The fruit isn't proof of your worth; it's evidence of grace at work.

Repentance may feel costly. It asks you to release old patterns that once felt like lifelines. But those patterns were chains. In turning from them, you're reclaiming freedom, hope, intimacy, and life.

## Asking God to Remove Character Defects

Addiction is rarely just about the substance or behavior itself; it's deeply rooted in the soil of the soul. Beneath the visible habits lie hidden forces: pride that masks pain, fear that drives escape, anger that erupts like wildfire, shame that festers in silence. These aren't merely personality quirks. They're the warped scaffolding that addiction often clings to.

In the language of many recovery communities, there's a step that reads, "Became entirely ready to have God remove all these defects of character."[5] This isn't about loathing the self, nor about achieving some spiritual perfection. It's a holy posture of willingness; a heart that opens its clenched fists and says, "God, here is what I can't change alone. Come and transform me."

In Christian spirituality, this process is referred to as sanctification.[6] It's not self-help. It's not striving. It's surrendering to the slow, steady work of the Holy Spirit. As Jesus taught in John 15, we're branches connected to a living vine. And the Father, the wise gardener, prunes us, not to punish but to make room for fruit. He cuts away what withers love and cultivates what gives life.

5. Alcoholics Anonymous, *Twelve Steps and Twelve Traditions*, 63.
6. Wesley, *Plain Account of Christian Perfection*.

So how do we do this? Begin by naming what's beneath the surface. Pray honestly: "God, show me the deeper patterns that feed my addiction. Reveal the pride, the fear, the impatience, the wounds." Then, ask boldly and humbly, "God, take them from me. Replace them with what's true and good and holy."

Scripture gives us a picture of what grows in a heart shaped by God: "Love, joy, peace, patience, kindness, goodness, faithfulness, gentleness, and self-control" (Gal 5:22–23). These fruits don't grow overnight. But the more we bring our defects before God (the more we admit, pray, and yield), the more space we create for divine transformation.

This isn't about becoming flawless. It's about becoming free. The defects of character that once ruled your inner world don't have to define your future. In Christ, the inner landscape can be reshaped. God isn't waiting for you to fix yourself. God is inviting you to be changed from within, as you walk hand-in-hand with the Spirit who heals, sanctifies, and restores.

## Seeking Deliverance from Spiritual Strongholds

Some chains are forged not just by habit, but by spiritual bondage.[7] Addiction isn't only a psychological or physiological phenomenon; sometimes it embeds itself in the spirit: in patterns so entrenched, in shadows so thick, they feel less like wounds and more like war. These are strongholds: lies believed for so long they calcify, behaviors repeated until they seem inevitable, spiritual oppressions that leave the soul gasping.

Scripture isn't silent on this. Ephesians 6 speaks of powers and principalities, of battles not waged merely against flesh and blood but against forces that seek to steal, kill, and destroy.[8] The good news is this: Christ has already conquered them. His resurrection isn't only a promise of life after death; it's a declaration of victory now, over every force that holds people captive.

So, what does deliverance look like for someone in recovery? It begins with recognizing the possibility. If you've tried everything (steps, strategies, support) and still feel ensnared, perhaps something deeper is at play. Maybe the roots aren't just in memory or mind, but in the spiritual realm.

This isn't to induce fear but to offer hope. Because there's real power available through prayer. Deliverance doesn't always mean an exorcism or dramatic event. Sometimes it's a quiet but firm prayer said aloud: "In the

7. Anderson, *Bondage Breaker.*

8. Eph 6:12; John 10:10.

name of Jesus, I break every agreement I've made with this addiction.[9] I renounce its hold. I belong to God, and God alone."

Sometimes it means asking others to pray over you, such as trusted pastors, spiritual mentors, or mature Christian friends. There's power in naming the bondage, repenting of any partnership with it, and calling on Jesus to break it. It might also involve confession, forgiveness, or renouncing specific acts or symbols tied to addiction (such as deleting apps, discarding objects, or removing access points that have become footholds for temptation).

This kind of prayer doesn't replace therapy, accountability, or wise counsel. It complements them. The healing of the soul must be comprehensive. Some wounds need balm. Others need chains broken.

And don't forget: You're not alone. The Spirit of God within you is greater than anything outside you. As 1 John 4:4 says, "The One who is in you is greater than the one who is in the world." When the enemy lies ("You'll never be free," "You're too far gone"), counter them with truth. Speak it. Stand in it. Clothe yourself in it, as Eph 6 describes: the belt of truth, the breastplate of righteousness, the shield of faith, the sword of the Spirit.

Deliverance isn't about hype. It's about holiness. It's the sacred act of reclaiming what belongs to God: you. It's about shedding the garments of shame and walking clothed in the authority of Christ.

## The Healing Power of Christ for Wounds

Addiction rarely appears out of nowhere. It often takes root in pain that has never been named or healed: wounds from childhood, betrayals that never mended, losses too vast for words. For me, addiction was deeply rooted in pain from my childhood and the emotional and psychological scars that had never healed. Many who find themselves in bondage to addiction are, in truth, wounded healers in search of healing.[10] And behind the substance or behavior lies a sorrow the soul couldn't bear alone.

This is why true recovery must include inner healing: not just from the actions, but from the ache. The gospel doesn't merely offer pardon for sin; it offers healing for brokenness. "He was pierced for our transgressions, crushed for our iniquities . . . and by his wounds we are healed" (Isa 53:5). These words weren't written only for the forgiveness of the guilty, but also for the healing of the bruised.

9. Kraft, *Defeating Dark Angels*.

10. Nouwen, *Wounded Healer*.

Jesus isn't distant from your pain. He carried it in his own body. He knows the sting of betrayal, the weight of rejection, the loneliness of nightfall. His resurrection doesn't only promise life beyond the grave, but healing for what feels like death within. He is both Savior and Healer. His love goes all the way into the wounded corners of your heart.

Consider inviting Christ into those places. In prayer, you might say, "Jesus, I welcome you into this memory. Into the moment I was hurt. Into the room where I learned to hide. Come and speak truth to the lies I believed. Come and show me where you were. Come and begin to heal what's still aching."

Sometimes this is done in silence, occasionally through tears, and for many people through guided prayer, journaling, or therapeutic support. The point isn't the method. The point is the presence. You aren't alone in your pain. And the places you've tried to numb are the very places Christ wants to restore.

Counseling or Christian therapy can be a sacred tool in this process. Don't think of therapy as a lack of faith. Think of it as an instrument of grace: a space where God often does profound healing through skilled, compassionate guides. Since recognizing my struggles with addiction, I've been in psychiatry, psychotherapy, and Christian counselling on and off for decades.[11] I can testify to its value and healing work.

And healing does come. Not always instantly. Not always completely in this life. But gradually, as you invite Christ into those memories and pains, something shifts. The inner torment lessens. The compulsions begin to fade. The behaviors you used to mask your wounds no longer feel necessary. Why? Because the wound itself is being tended to by divine hands.

Psalm 147:3 says, "God heals the brokenhearted and binds up their wounds." That promise isn't poetic exaggeration. It's a reality. God sees the wounded places in you. And God won't walk past them. Christ enters your pain, not to fix you overnight, but to heal you deeply, and tell you that your worth was never based on your pain, your failures, or your addictions. You are beloved. And love is stronger than trauma.

## Accountability and Confession to Others

Healing is personal, but it's never private. The road out of addiction requires community, courage, and confession: not just to God, but to others. We weren't meant to walk this road alone. And shame, that cruel and

11. May, *Addiction and Grace.*

persistent companion of addiction, loses its power when exposed to the light of shared honesty.

James 5:16 says, "Confess your sins to one another and pray for one another so that you may be healed." That's not a suggestion. It's a spiritual truth. There is healing in honest confession. There is freedom in being known. When we hide our struggles, they tighten their grip. But when we speak them aloud to someone we trust, we create space for grace to enter.

This isn't about airing your soul to everyone. It's about finding safe people: those who will listen without judgment, who will speak truth in love, who will hold your story with care. Maybe it's a sponsor, a pastor, a friend, or someone in your recovery group. The identity of the person matters less than their trustworthiness and grace.

Confessing to another person is hard. It requires humility. It strips away the masks. But it also brings immense relief. You no longer must carry your secrets alone. You no longer must pretend you're fine. In that moment of confession, you step into the light. And where there is light, there is less shame. Less isolation. More truth. More healing.

Accountability naturally follows from this. When someone knows your struggle, they can check in. They can celebrate your victories and walk with you through setbacks. They can remind you of who you are when you forget. They can pray for you and with you. That kind of support isn't weakness; it's strength. It's a picture of the body of Christ, bearing one another's burdens, and so fulfilling the law of love.[12]

Don't wait for perfection to open up. Confess in your mess. That's where the power of grace shines brightest. And if you've been burned by people in the past (if your story of confession includes pain or betrayal), know that not every person is safe, but some are. Pray for discernment. And when you find someone trustworthy, take the risk to be honest.

You were never meant to walk this road alone. God designed us for companionship in the struggle and community in the healing. In confession and accountability, your story becomes a shared one, and in that sharing, shame loses its voice, and hope begins to rise.

## Embracing a Clean Conscience

A miracle unfolds in our soul when we truly receive forgiveness. It's not loud or flashy, but it changes everything. Scripture says, "Let us draw near with a sincere heart and with the full assurance that faith brings, having our hearts sprinkled to cleanse us from a guilty conscience" (Heb 10:22). Those

12. Gal 6:2.

words aren't abstract. They're water for the parched. This is holy and good news, for the one whose past is heavy with shame and for the one who has sat in the rubble of broken promises and weary relapses.

Addiction often trains a person to live in the shadows, ducking beneath guilt, performing for love, burying regret. But the cross doesn't offer a new performance; it offers a new heart. And part of that newness is the cleansing of the conscience. The memory of the past may linger, but its sting begins to fade when it's bathed in grace.

A clean conscience isn't earned by being good enough. It's received by trusting in the one who's good. Jesus bore the weight of our guilt so we wouldn't have to carry it anymore. That's not a spiritual cliché, it's a liberation. The blood of Christ doesn't just cancel sin's record; it cleanses its residue from the soul.[13] This is the part so many in recovery struggle to believe. They think, "Sure, maybe God forgives me, but I still feel stained." And here the invitation must be gently, yet firmly, restated: believe the gospel not only with your theology and mind but with your heart and body.

This doesn't mean forgetting everything, nor pretending that wounds didn't happen. But it means refusing to let the past define who you are now. Grace doesn't erase memory, but it rewrites meaning.[14] You're no longer "dirty," "ruined," or "beyond help." You're washed. You're new. You're no longer under condemnation. You can hold your head high, not out of pride but out of freedom.

Shame thrives in hidden places. But when brought into the light, it begins to die. With a clean conscience, you can begin to breathe again. No more proving yourself. No more penance. No more measuring yourself against an impossible standard. The slate is clean. And from this place of peace, the journey of sobriety and healing takes on new power, not because you're trying to escape guilt but because you're finally walking in love.

So, if guilt still clings to you like smoke after a fire, return again to the altar of grace. Let the Spirit speak to your inner being: "You're forgiven. You're clean. You're mine." Let that truth echo until it becomes your truest name.

## Building New Foundations

When walls have crumbled and the roof has caved in, what's left is the ground beneath your feet. That's where God begins. The spiritual work of confession and repentance isn't about managing sin or tidying up failure. It's about clearing away the debris so something new can be built. And

13. Heb 9:14; 10:22.

14. Volf, *End of Memory*.

what's being built now is a life founded on truth, transparency, and trust in divine mercy.

Confession tears down the walls of denial. Repentance reorients your steps. Together, they form the concrete slab of a new life: one that's no longer constructed from secrecy and self-reliance, but from honesty and grace. This new foundation doesn't erase the past, but it does change what's possible in the future.

Recovery isn't just about abstaining from a harmful substance or behavior. It's about rebuilding your whole way of living. With this clean slate, this new starting ground, you're now invited to construct a life that's different: one choice, one day, one moment of surrender at a time. This foundation is strong not because you built it with perfect materials, but because it rests on Christ's mercy, not your own merit.[15]

One of the most vital habits to develop now is the practice of keeping "short accounts" with God. Don't let unconfessed sin or silent shame pile up. When you stumble (and you will) confess quickly. Run to grace rather than away from it. This practice keeps the foundation clear. It makes spiritual maintenance part of the architecture of your life. In recovery, this habit matters. Guilt can become a trapdoor back into old patterns if not quickly addressed.[16] But when you get used to bringing everything (failures, victories, confusion, longing) before God daily, you remain grounded. You don't spiral as easily. You don't hide.

Looking ahead, you'll begin to engage with the relational dimensions of recovery: forgiveness, amends, reconciliation. But you can't offer what you haven't received. By embracing the forgiveness of God and standing firmly on this new foundation, you're preparing your heart to face others: not defensively but honestly, not with excuses but with humility, and not with shame but with courage.

This work matters more than you can know. Foundations determine what can be built on top. The deeper you go in grace, the taller you can grow in wholeness. This isn't about self-improvement. It's about becoming rooted in a new identity: the beloved child of God, the one being rebuilt not in your own strength but by divine hands.

So, take a breath. Look around. You've laid something holy. The old life may have collapsed, but something far better is being constructed. You're not who you were. And the ground beneath your feet (this truth, this grace, this God) is solid. Pause here, and let grace settle deep: what was once buried in shame is now rooted in mercy, and a new foundation is being laid beneath your feet.

15. 1 Cor 3:11.

16. May, *Addiction and Grace.*

## Reflection Questions

1. Where in my life have I experienced the gentle conviction of God leading me toward confession and healing?
2. What specific sins, regrets, or wounds have I hesitated to bring fully into the light of God's presence?
3. How have I experienced the difference between guilt that leads to repentance and shame that leads to hiding?
4. What does it mean to me personally to believe that God isn't only willing but eager to forgive and cleanse me?
5. In what ways might I still be holding onto secrecy or self-condemnation, and how can I invite God's truth into those places?

## Action Steps

1. Take thirty minutes in quiet prayer to confess specific sins or painful memories to God, trusting in divine mercy and cleansing.
2. Write a prayer of repentance in your journal, naming areas of struggle and asking God to begin transforming your heart and habits.
3. If you feel ready, share one of your hidden struggles with a trusted spiritual mentor, pastor, or recovery friend this week.
4. Meditate on 1 John 1:9 or Ps 51 each day for the next five days, and reflect on what it means to be made clean.

# 5.

# Grace and Forgiveness

## Receiving Mercy, Extending Mercy

Some wounds leave no visible scars, but their weight lingers deep within the soul. To walk the path of healing is to encounter mercy. This is a mercy that meets us in our guilt, lifts the burden of shame, and teaches us how to forgive as we have been forgiven.

### Living in God's Grace Instead of Guilt

Grace isn't a doctrine to memorize but a homecoming to live in. It's the outstretched arm of God meeting the soul weighed down by regret and saying, "Come, rest here." For those on the long road of recovery, guilt often clings like a second skin. It says that the past defines you, that you've gone too far, stayed too long in the shadows, failed one too many times. But grace sings louder: You're forgiven, cleansed, and dearly loved.

The journey toward freedom begins in the soil of grace. It's not earned or deserved. It's lavished: poured out without measure by a God who knows every wound and every relapse and yet still welcomes you with open arms. Psalm 103 declares that God removes our sins "as far as the east is from the west," and this is no metaphorical sentiment. It's the architecture of salvation. When Christ said, "It's finished," it was a declaration that no more penance is needed.[1] The cross was enough.

1. John 19:30.

But guilt is persistent. It doesn't always leave when sin does. It lingers, disguising itself as humility or self-awareness, suggesting that real healing means continuing to punish yourself. Don't believe this lie. Guilt that remains after grace isn't holy. It's a chain the enemy forges from half-truths and shame. The truth is that you now stand in grace. Romans 5:2 reminds us we "have gained access by faith into this grace in which we now stand." To stand in grace means to reject the voice of condemnation and to feel instead the presence of divine mercy.

This isn't a naïve ignoring of the past. It's a re-narrating of it through the lens of redemption. Every scar can become a testimony: every failure, a signpost pointing to divine mercy. Daily, remind yourself: "I'm no longer under condemnation. I'm under grace."[2] Write it down. Pray it aloud. Believe it in your bones. Living in grace doesn't mean forgetting what you've done: it means remembering who has redeemed you. Let joy rise where shame once reigned. Let gratitude take the place of guilt. This isn't self-help optimism. This is resurrection living.

## Forgiving Yourself

Forgiveness is a seed planted in the soil of grace, but for many, it never seems to grow roots within the self. Even when someone believes that God forgives them, they may still live with a relentless inner critic: a voice that won't let them forget, won't let them breathe, and won't let them heal. But forgiving yourself isn't self-indulgence; it's agreement with God's truth.

When you refuse to forgive yourself, you subtly place your judgment above God's. You declare (perhaps unconsciously) that Christ's sacrifice was insufficient. But the gospel insists otherwise. The blood of Jesus speaks a better word than your shame ever could.[3] It says you're clean. You're beloved. You're made new. This isn't earned through apology or discipline; it's received like light upon the face at dawn.

Many in addiction recovery struggle to believe this because they've hurt others. They've broken promises, relationships, and even themselves. But the grace that forgives is also the grace that restores. God isn't just concerned with your past actions but with your becoming. You're not only forgiven; you're being made whole.

The practice of self-forgiveness often begins with how you speak to yourself. When a shameful memory rises, don't spiral into self-condemnation. Pause. Breathe. Pray: "Thank you, God, that I'm forgiven. Thank

2. Rom 8:1.

3. Heb 12:24.

you for who I am now. Thank you for being my beloved." Let your mind be trained in grace. Let your self-talk become gospel-soaked.

Try this: Write a letter to your addicted self, not with blame, but with compassion. Speak words of grace. Tell that version of you what God has told you. Then release it, burn it, bury it, or offer it. Let the act be both symbolic and sacred. You're not that person anymore. You're being transformed.

Forgiving yourself doesn't mean forgetting. It means holding memory in the light of mercy. It means choosing not to use your past to harm yourself. The One who knows all things has chosen to cast your sins into the depths of the sea.[4] Who are you to go fishing?

You were made for freedom. And part of that freedom is silencing the lie that you're unworthy of it. Begin again. And again. And again. God's grace has no quota. And your healing doesn't require your self-hatred; it requires your surrender.

## Understanding What Forgiveness Is and Isn't

Forgiveness is one of the most misunderstood, misused, and misrepresented gifts in the spiritual life. Many carry wounds so deep, betrayals so raw, they flinch at the word. It's no wonder. Too often, forgiveness has been equated with denial, silence, or forced reconciliation. But true forgiveness is none of these things. It isn't a denial of justice, nor an invitation to be harmed again. It isn't the erasure of memory or the acceptance of abuse. It's, instead, the fierce choice to unclench the fists of the soul.

Forgiveness doesn't excuse wrongdoing. It names the harm honestly and thoroughly. It doesn't say, "It was nothing." It says, "It was devastating, and I choose not to be defined by it." It isn't forgetting; it's remembering differently. Forgiveness is the release of the right to get even. It's placing the weight of justice in God's hands and saying, "You are wiser and fairer than I'll ever be. I trust you, my God, with this."[5]

Forgiveness doesn't always restore a relationship. Sometimes it can, but not always. Reconciliation requires repentance and mutual trust; forgiveness doesn't. You can forgive and still maintain boundaries. You can forgive and still say no. You can forgive and never speak to the person again, not out of hate but out of wisdom and safety. Think of it like this: if someone once stole your wallet, forgiveness means you let go of the need to punish them, but it doesn't mean you leave your wallet on the table next time.[6]

4. Mic 7:19.

5. Rom 12:19.

6. This metaphor is widely attributed to Smedes, *Forgive and Forget*, 135. While

When Jesus taught forgiveness, he never minimized pain. He simply insisted it wouldn't have the final word. Forgiveness isn't weakness; it's strength. It isn't passive; it's active, liberating the forgiver from being tethered forever to the harm. Unforgiveness chains us to the one who wronged us. Forgiveness cuts the cord.[7] It says, "I won't let this control me any longer."

To forgive is to be free. Not to forget. Not to excuse. Not to open oneself up to more suffering. But to walk forward unburdened, healed, and whole. This is the road Christ invites us to walk: slowly, prayerfully, honestly.

## Confronting Resentments

Resentment is a slow poison. It hides in the corners of memory, feeding on betrayal, bitterness, and pain. For many who battle addiction, resentment is both a companion and a chain. It justifies self-destruction, stokes the fire of anger, and becomes a convenient reason not to heal. But if we're to move forward in recovery, we must face our resentments with courage and clarity.

Begin here: make a list. Make this list a brutal, honest inventory of those you still carry bitterness toward (family, exes, bosses, church leaders, abusers, even God). Yes, even God. Name them. Don't edit yourself. Write down what they did, how it hurt, and why it still stings. This isn't an exercise in blame. It's an invitation to clarity. You can't forgive what you refuse to name.

And as you name them, notice something: how your body feels, where your heart clenches, where your mind drifts. Resentment takes up residence in the body. It causes insomnia, stress, and disease. It feeds addiction. Many people use substances because they are angry and don't know what to do with their emotions. But Scripture speaks directly to this: "Get rid of all bitterness, rage and anger. . . . Be kind and compassionate to one another, forgiving each other, just as in Christ God forgave you" (Eph 4:31–32). Forgiveness isn't just a spiritual act; it's a healing one. Forgiveness is a detox of the soul and a liberation of the spirit.

But here's the truth: You may not feel ready to forgive. That's okay. Start by asking for the willingness to forgive. Pray for the desire to let go, even if you're not ready yet. Forgiveness is often a process, not a moment. First, you name the hurt. Then you sit with it. Then you begin to release it: not all at once, but bit by bit, like draining poison from a wound.

This is hard, sacred work. It may take weeks, months, or years. But every time you choose to bless instead of curse, to pray instead of plot, to release instead of rehearse, you are being set free. Forgiveness isn't just for

---

the exact phrasing varies, the concept originates in his writings.

7. Smedes, *Forgive and Forget*, 4–5.

them; it's for you. Resentment holds you hostage to someone else's actions. Forgiveness sets the hostage free, and you'll discover the hostage was you.

In the battle for sobriety and healing, resentment is a land mine. Disarm it. Don't let the one who hurt you also destroy your present peace. Let God hold the justice. Let grace do its slow and holy work.

## Choosing to Forgive: The Act of the Will

Forgiveness rarely begins with a rush of warm feelings. It starts with a choice, a deliberate act of the will that says, "I'll no longer carry this debt. I won't allow this wrong to define me or poison my soul." You may still feel the sting, the ache, even the outrage, but you choose forgiveness before you feel it. This is the way of Christ. On the cross, in the grip of agony, Jesus didn't wait for an apology. He said, "Father, forgive them, for they don't know what they're doing."[8] That was no accident of timing; it was a deliberate act of mercy at the moment of deepest pain.

Sometimes we need to make this choice tangible. Write a letter to the person you're forgiving, not to send but to name the harm, the loss, the grief. Write "I choose to forgive you" somewhere in that letter. Then burn it, shred it, bury it; whatever helps you embody the release. You can also speak the forgiveness aloud in prayer, saying, "God, before you, I forgive this person for what they said or did." Name the offense. This naming is part of the cleansing.

Forgiveness is rarely a one-time act. Wounds have layers, and sometimes the same hurt resurfaces months or years later. That's normal. When the bitterness rises again, choose again. Forgive again. Not because the offense grows smaller, but because you refuse to let it grow roots in your soul. Forgiveness is like peeling away shackles one link at a time.

Jesus taught, "Forgive, and you will be forgiven."[9] This isn't a transaction, but an invitation into the flow of grace. Those who receive mercy become channels of mercy. Each choice to forgive is an act of holy rebellion against the forces that would keep you chained to the past. It's you saying, "I won't remain a victim of what happened. I'll walk in the freedom God offers me." Forgiveness, in the end, isn't about excusing them; it's about freeing you.

8. Luke 23:34.
9. Luke 6:37.

## Seeking God's Help to Forgive the Deep Wounds

Some wounds run so deep they defy human willpower. Abuse. Betrayal. Violence. These aren't paper cuts of the soul, they're fractures that change you. To even suggest forgiveness here can feel impossible, even offensive, unless we're speaking of something greater than human effort. This is where forgiveness moves from a human choice to a supernatural work of grace.

God never asks us to pretend deep wounds aren't deep. Scripture doesn't dismiss grief or deny injustice; it acknowledges them. The Bible invites us to bring our raw, unfiltered pain to God. Tell God the truth: "I can't forgive this. It feels too big, too evil, too deliberate." Name the anger, the confusion, the grief. There's no shame in admitting the limits of your strength. The One who calls you to forgive also promises, "My grace is sufficient for you, for my power is made perfect in weakness."[10]

Philippians 4:13 ("I can do all this through him who gives me strength") wasn't written for easy victories. It was written for the moments that demand divine intervention. For the days when you can't even imagine letting go of the anger, much less wishing your offender well. And yet, that's often where the journey begins, not with feeling different but with praying differently. "God, I'm not ready to forgive. But I'm willing for you to make me willing. Do in me what I can't do for myself."

Sometimes that prayer will be the only thing you can manage for a season. At other times, you may take the small but defiant step of praying for your offender's good, not in a forced or sugary way, but as an act of obedience. You might say, "God, I release this person to you. I pray your will for them, whatever that may be." You aren't excusing the harm. You're entrusting it to the only Judge who sees every angle and weighs every heart.

Stories abound of people who, by God's Spirit, forgave what seemed unforgivable: a murderer's mother who embraced the man who killed her son, or a survivor praying blessing over her abuser.[11] These aren't the triumphs of human niceness; they're miracles of divine mercy working through fragile human vessels.

When you hand your deep wounds to God, you aren't simply giving up a grudge; you're inviting the Healer into the most guarded room of your soul. Over time, you may find that the very place you thought would remain a scar forever becomes a source of strength, even compassion, for others. Forgiveness here isn't a denial of the past; it's a declaration that the past won't have the final say.

10. 2 Cor 12:9.

11. See Tutu and Tutu, *Book of Forgiving*, 187–90, for examples of radical forgiveness in post-apartheid South Africa and beyond.

## Experiencing Freedom from Bitterness

Bitterness is a silent captor. I've known its poison and power, as it's seeped into my heart and corrupted my relationships and spirituality. Bitterness binds the heart with invisible chains, feeding off the memory of wrongs and keeping the soul in a perpetual posture of defense. For many, bitterness feels like a shield, something that protects against further harm. But over time, it corrodes from the inside out. It seeps into speech, poisons relationships, and robs people of joy. Bitterness promises the moral high ground, but leaves us with dulled moral and ethical sensitivities, and a reduced chance of demonstrating to the world what integrity and mercy look like. Bitterness becomes a slow-acting toxin that reshapes one's identity, until they're known less for who they are and more for what they resent.

People who forgive often describe a physical sensation, as if something heavy has been lifted from their chest. They speak of clarity returning, of laughter feeling easier, of sleeping through the night without rehearsing arguments or re-living scenes. This isn't wishful thinking. The human mind and body weren't designed to hold bitterness indefinitely.[12] Letting it go releases energy once spent on fueling anger and guarding the wound. That energy can be reallocated to living, creating, and loving.

Forgiveness isn't naïve; it's courageous. It's saying, "I refuse to be defined by the harm done to me." It breaks the cause-and-effect chain that ties the present to the past. In recovery, this freedom can reduce triggers dramatically, because anger and unhealed pain are often what drove us to numb ourselves in the first place. When bitterness is gone, the compulsion to medicate that bitterness loses its power.

A truth worth holding: "Forgiveness sets a prisoner free and reveals that the prisoner was you."[13]

This freedom isn't fragile; it's resilient. It doesn't mean you'll never feel anger again, but it does mean that anger won't own you. Over time, you may even find the capacity to bless the one who harmed you: not because they deserve it, but because you no longer need to protect yourself with hatred. You've found a better shelter.

12. Mayo Clinic Staff, "Forgiveness."

13. This concept is widely attributed to Lewis B. Smedes. See Smedes, *Forgive and Forget*, 93.

## Resting in God's Justice

One of the deepest resistances to forgiveness is the fear that by letting go, we allow injustice to win. Something in us clings to the ledger, keeping score, because releasing the debt feels like erasing the truth. This is why so many stay locked in unforgiveness: it feels safer to keep the evidence close, to maintain control over the narrative.

But Scripture reminds us that justice isn't our burden to carry. Romans 12:19 says plainly, "'It's mine to avenge; I'll repay,' says the Lord." This isn't a call to vindictiveness on God's part, but an invitation for us to step out from under the crushing weight of being our own avenger. Forgiveness isn't pretending the wrong didn't happen; it's placing the case into the hands of the only Judge who sees every detail, motive, and ripple effect.

When we forgive, we aren't excusing injustice; we're entrusting it. God's justice is neither careless nor delayed; it's perfectly timed and perfectly measured. Sometimes that justice is restorative, bringing repentance and healing to the one who harmed us. Sometimes it's corrective, restraining their actions or exposing the harm they've done. But it's always just.

There's also a theological grounding here that can't be ignored: We forgive because God has forgiven us. Jesus told the parable of the unforgiving servant (Matt 18:21–35) to show the absurdity of receiving immeasurable mercy and then refusing to extend even a fraction of it to others. We're all debtors whose accounts have been cleared by grace. When we keep this in view, the offense against us (however real and painful) takes its place in proportion to the mercy we have already received.

Resting in God's justice frees us from rehearsing revenge in our minds. It silences the "what if" and "if only" loops that keep us stuck. It also releases us from the exhausting task of trying to manage both healing and judgment simultaneously. Healing requires openness; judgment requires constant vigilance. We can't do both.

When you place justice in God's hands, you step into a deeper kind of rest. It's the rest that comes from knowing you're no longer the keeper of the scales. You can focus on becoming whole, while trusting that the One who holds the universe together will also hold every wrong to account. This rest isn't passivity; it's trust in action. And in that trust, the seeds of peace can take root.

## Grace for Others, Grace for Yourself

Grace is the atmosphere of the kingdom, the breath of new life. It isn't earned, bartered, or negotiated; it's given. We have been welcomed into this grace not because we were strong enough to fix ourselves, but because God met us in our weakness and refused to let go.[14] The same hand that lifted us from the pit still holds us steady on this path. To live in that reality is to become a person who carries grace everywhere we go.

Grace for others begins with the recognition that we've been forgiven of far more than we'll ever be asked to forgive. The offense someone committed against us may feel profound and unforgettable, but we know our own story: we see the wreckage we've left behind. And yet, God's mercy didn't withhold forgiveness until we proved ourselves worthy; it came to us while we were still entangled in our mess. If that's how heaven deals with our failings, can we not learn to offer a fraction of that mercy to those around us?

Grace for yourself is equally essential, although it's often harder to extend to others. Many in recovery find it easier to forgive others than to stop punishing themselves. But holding onto self-condemnation is like re-sentencing yourself after the judge has declared you free. To walk in grace is to accept, fully and daily, that your identity is no longer "addict," "failure," or "unworthy," but "beloved," "redeemed," and "new creation."[15]

This grace becomes a cycle that dismantles the cycle of hurt. When we respond to others with mercy rather than retaliation, we interrupt patterns of generational resentment. When we treat ourselves with compassion instead of shame, we model for others what it looks like to live without the weight of condemnation. Over time, this shifts the atmosphere of our relationships, our homes, and even our communities.

If you listen to some testosterone-filled Christian podcasters, you'd think grace, mercy, and empathy are weaknesses. But these qualities aren't softness, they're strength.[16] Grace isn't weakness; it's the fierce strength to respond to sin with forgiveness instead of vengeance, to greet stumbling with a hand up instead of a push down. Grace isn't a single event but a daily practice. Every new day offers opportunities to choose grace again: toward the person who cuts you off in traffic, toward the coworker who misunderstands you, toward the family member who reopens old wounds, and toward yourself when you falter.

14. Rom 5:6–8.

15. 2 Cor 5:17.

16. Eph 2:8–9; Alcoholics Anonymous, *Alcoholics Anonymous*, 83–84.

To live in grace is to refuse to let bitterness set the tone for your life. Grace is the slow, steady breaking of old chains and the careful crafting of a new legacy: one that leaves behind peace instead of resentment, freedom instead of bondage, and love instead of fear.[17]

Pause here, and let grace breathe through you, settling the heart, loosening the grip of the past, and opening your hands to the freedom already given.

## Reflection Questions

1. Where have I most clearly experienced God's grace in my recovery journey so far?
2. What thoughts or feelings still make it hard for me to accept God's forgiveness for my past fully?
3. How do I usually respond when guilt resurfaces? Do I turn toward grace or away from it?
4. In what ways might forgiving myself open the door for more profound healing and restored relationships?
5. Which Scripture from this chapter speaks most powerfully to my need for grace today, and why?

## Action Steps

1. Each morning this week, begin your day by thanking God for one specific way divine grace has met you in your recovery.
2. When a memory or feeling of guilt arises, pause to pray a short prayer of release: "Thank you, Lord, that I'm forgiven and free in you."
3. Write down one way you can show grace to yourself and one way you can extend grace to someone else in the coming week.
4. Choose one verse from this chapter about forgiveness or grace to memorize and repeat it whenever shame or self-condemnation begins to surface.

17. Gal 5:1; 1 John 4:18.

# 6.

# Rebuilding Relationships

## Making Amends and Restoration

The path of recovery is never walked alone. Love, once fractured by addiction, can be mended by grace. In the hands of God, even the most broken relationships can become testimonies of redemption.[1]

### Assessing the Wreckage

Recovery isn't just about the harm done to ourselves; it's also about facing, with honesty and humility, the harm our choices have inflicted on others. Addiction doesn't operate in isolation. Its reach is like a spill of oil on water: silent but far-reaching, staining everything it touches. Families feel it in the weight of broken trust. Friends notice the distance growing between shared laughter and awkward silences. Employers see it in missed deadlines or compromised integrity. Children carry it in ways they may not have the words to express. As I think about the wreckage caused by my alcoholism, I'm heartbroken and grateful to my family who've forgiven me for all I've said and done.

Assessing the wreckage means pausing to name these impacts. It may help to make a list, not to wallow in guilt but to open the door toward repair.[2] Who was hurt by your actions? What specific choices contributed to that harm? Did it come through deception, neglect, volatility, financial misuse,

1. 2 Cor 5:18–19.
2. Alcoholics Anonymous, *Alcoholics Anonymous*, 59–60.

or emotional withdrawal? Writing these down can be painful; shame may flare up, and the temptation to minimize may whisper in your ear. Resist the urge to turn away. This isn't an exercise in self-condemnation, but in truth-telling.

This inventory is outward-focused, yet it inevitably stirs inward reflection. We begin to see not only the acts themselves but the patterns that fueled them. Perhaps our anger spilled over onto those who loved us most. Possibly, our isolation left others feeling abandoned. Perhaps we sought relief in substances when we should have sought help. These acknowledgments bring a sober clarity that's necessary for growth.

In the language of recovery, this step is a bridge between personal transformation and relational restoration.[3] Without it, attempts at amends risk being shallow or self-serving. With it, our words of apology carry weight because they are informed by honest recognition of the damage done.

The process also prepares us emotionally. Facing the reality of our impact helps us approach those conversations with humility rather than defensiveness. We aren't coming to argue over who was more at fault, but to take full ownership of our part. Even if reconciliation isn't possible in every relationship, this work frees us from denial and positions us to live differently in the future.

Assessing the wreckage isn't easy, but it's sacred work. It aligns with the God who invites us into the light, not to shame us but to heal us.[4] And it lays the groundwork for the following steps: making amends where possible, setting right what can be set right, and walking in a way that no longer leaves new wreckage in our wake.

## Taking Ownership of Your Actions

Recovery calls us to the deep work of honesty, the kind that refuses to hide behind shadows, excuses, or carefully rehearsed lines. It's tempting to protect ourselves by saying, "It wasn't really me, it was the addiction." We hope that separating ourselves from the harm will somehow make the guilt lighter, the wounds less painful. But that path is an illusion. Healing grows only in the soil of truth. And the truth is that, even when we were sick, trapped, or desperate, our choices still carried weight. They rippled out into the lives of others, sometimes in ways we may never fully know.

Taking ownership isn't about condemning yourself or locking your soul in shame. It's about stepping fully into the light where grace does its

3. Matt 5:23–24.

4. 1 John 1:7.

best and most transformative work.[5] To take responsibility is to speak plainly, without embellishment or qualification: "I did this. It was wrong. I regret it." Words like these carry the weight of humility and the power of disarmingly truth. They close the door on self-justification and open the way toward trust. By contrast, excuses or half-measures, like "If I hurt you, I'm sorry," often sound hollow, offering neither clarity nor comfort to the one who has been wounded.

Owning the truth will come at a cost. It may cost your pride, your illusion of control, or your ability to tell yourself a softer version of your story. But it's a cost worth paying, because it rebuilds what dishonesty and denial have destroyed.

There's a holy dignity in this posture. It says, I'm willing to be seen for who I am (with my failures and all), because I believe there's more to my story than my mistakes.[6] It's a declaration that you no longer need to live in the shadows, and that you trust God's grace to be big enough to hold the whole truth about you. Those who hear your confession may not be ready to forgive, and that's okay. The point isn't to control their reaction but to walk in integrity regardless.

Over time, sincerity in owning your actions becomes a testimony in itself. It tells the world you're no longer hiding, no longer content to live half-truths, but willing to face the past so that a different future can take root. This is the beginning of reconciliation: not always its end, but always its seed, and a seed that, when nurtured, can grow into peace, restoration, and freedom.[7]

## Understanding Amends—More Than Apologies

Making amends is more than uttering the words "I'm sorry." Apologies matter, but in recovery they're only the doorway, not the whole house. To amend something is to restore what has been broken, to repair what has been damaged, to return what has been taken. It's an act of integrity that blends humility with tangible action. Words alone can soothe for a moment, but actions confirm that the words are true.

In Scripture, this is embodied in the story of Zacchaeus.[8] When Jesus met him, Zacchaeus didn't just confess his wrongs; he offered restitution, repaying what he had taken, and even going beyond what the law

5. 1 John 1:7.
6. 2 Cor 5:17.
7. Matt 5:23–24.
8. Luke 19:1–10.

required. His generosity was proof that his heart had truly changed. Similarly, making amends in recovery is an outward manifestation of an inward transformation.

Amends can take many forms. Sometimes it means paying back money owed or replacing property damaged. At other times, it may require investing time to rebuild trust with someone who has been neglected or hurt. It could mean writing a heartfelt letter, offering a sincere conversation, or even performing an act of service to demonstrate goodwill. There'll be moments when full restitution isn't possible—perhaps the person is no longer alive or reconciliation would cause further harm. In those cases, amends can still be made symbolically: donating to a cause in their honor, doing good for others in a similar situation, or making a private act of commitment to live differently.

True amends flow from a heart that has stopped defending itself and is willing to bear the discomfort of making things right. You aren't seeking to earn forgiveness or clear your conscience at someone else's expense. You're showing that you value the relationship enough to repair what you can.

Making amends is often slow work. Some will receive your effort with warmth; others may still be cautious or even reject it. That's not failure. The act of reaching out, of humbling yourself, of putting repair into motion: these are victories in themselves. The outcome isn't yours to control; the faithfulness of your effort is.

In recovery, amends are a bridge: sometimes to reconciliation, sometimes simply to closure. Either way, they help dismantle the lingering guilt and regret that can feed relapse. They tell the world, and your heart, that you're not only leaving the old life behind but also actively restoring what you can from the damage it caused. This is the gospel lived out in real time—grace received becoming grace offered, in word, heart, and deed.[9]

## Preparing to Apologize Sincerely

A good apology is more than a polite formality or an offer of words; it's an act of humility, an open door for grace to walk through.[10] Many people have never been taught how to apologize well. They mumble vague admissions, hide behind humor, or pad the truth with excuses. So, the moment passes without real connection. I don't remember being taught how to apologize well when I was young. Perhaps you had the same experience. Instead of apologies, I saw people justifying their actions, offering excuses, or

9. Eph 4:32.

10. Chapman and Thomas, *Five Languages of Apology.*

throwing the blame onto others or even the person being apologized to. But a sincere apology, like living water poured onto parched ground, can soften even the hardest soil. Such an apology begins with clarity—name what you did wrong plainly.[11] No softening, no hedging, no "mistakes were made." Speak truth in simple words, letting them carry the weight they should.

Next, acknowledge the impact. It's not enough to confess the action; you must name the wound it left. "When I missed your graduation, you felt abandoned and unimportant. I see now how that hurt you." This step honors the other person's reality instead of rushing past their pain. After that, express genuine remorse. The person you're speaking with should see that your tone and posture convey that you're not simply checking a box but genuinely feeling the sorrow of what happened.

If it's appropriate, describe what you're doing to change. Don't make grand promises, which rarely hold up. Instead, describe the practical things you're doing to change, such as attending recovery meetings, keeping accountability, and setting boundaries. Sometimes you may also ask what you can do to make it right. Be ready to hear the answer without defensiveness.

Leave out the "but." That single word can undo an entire apology. "I'm sorry I shouted, but you were provoking me" places the blame right back on the other person and undermines the sincerity of your words. If you feel tempted to justify, swallow the urge and let your apology stand without conditions.

For some, it helps to write the apology before speaking it. Putting words on paper forces clarity and allows you to examine your heart before stepping into the conversation. Timing matters too. Pray for discernment, and seek counsel from a trusted mentor or sponsor about when and how to approach someone.[12] Avoid moments of crisis or public gatherings. Choose a time that gives space for listening, reflection, and grace.

When approached this way, an apology becomes more than a transaction: it becomes a holy offering, and a way of saying, "I see the harm I've caused, and I honor you enough to face it." Even before you speak, such preparation shapes your heart into a posture of peace and humility.

## Facing the People You've Hurt

There's a deep ache in the stomach when you think about meeting the eyes of someone you've wronged. Shame rises like a wave, threatening to pull you back into the shadows. I know what that's like. You're filled with fear,

11. Alcoholics Anonymous, *Twelve Steps and Twelve Traditions*, 77–83.

12. Haugk, *Christian Caregiving*, 93–102.

anxiety, and shame, and can be overwhelmed with these emotions. But this is also the place where chains break. Facing the people you've hurt isn't only for their healing; it's for yours. It's a declaration that you refuse to be ruled by fear or avoidance any longer.

Expect the anxiety. It's natural. Breathe through it and remember: This step isn't about winning approval, clearing your name, or forcing reconciliation. It's about walking in truth. You're not responsible for the other person's reaction, only for your integrity.[13] That can be a hard posture and attitude to take, especially if you're desperate for reconciliation. But God's grace and power are available to you.

Sometimes it helps to begin with less intimidating situations, such as someone with whom the offense was smaller or the relationship is already on the mend. Early successes build courage. In other cases, you may need a trusted friend, sponsor, or mentor to accompany you for support (or the other person may request the same). Their presence can keep you grounded, especially if the conversation turns heated or emotional.

Be prepared for a range of responses. Some may meet you with gratitude, surprised and relieved by your humility. Others may react with anger or disbelief, unwilling to trust that you've truly changed. Still others may weep, not in condemnation but in the release of long-held pain. Each response is valid; each is outside your control.

Go in with no demands. Don't go into the conversation with any expectation of instant forgiveness, and don't insist that the relationship return to what it once was. Sometimes your amends will open a new chapter of connection. Sometimes it will simply be a closing of the book, a final act of peace that releases both of you to move on.

Hold onto this truth: The act of showing up is, in itself, a victory. Walking toward someone with honesty is a declaration of freedom from the old ways of hiding, blaming, or numbing. Even if the other person refuses your apology, you have still honored the truth and taken responsibility. That seed will bear fruit in you, and perhaps in them, in ways you can't yet see.

Facing those you've hurt is one of the most courageous steps in recovery. It calls you to stand in the open, unarmed and unguarded, trusting that the God who began a good work in you will carry it forward. Whether the encounter ends in tears, silence, or embrace, you leave with a lighter heart, knowing you have done what is right. That, in itself, is a form of healing.

13. Alcoholics Anonymous, *Twelve Steps and Twelve Traditions*, 80–81.

## When Apologies Aren't Accepted

Sometimes, reconciliation remains out of reach. Hearts may still be guarded, and wounds may still be raw. You can't force another to receive what you offer. Your calling is to walk in truth, humbly and without demand, trusting that sowing seeds of peace is never wasted in the soil of hearts, lives, and eternity.[14] There are times when we may feel that forgiveness or remorse is wasted, but they aren't. Even if our forgiveness, sorrow, or repentance are unseen, they nurture faith, hope, and love in our hearts, and set our lives on the trajectory of discipleship. God will give you peace in your spirit by divine grace, although that peace may come and go in your heart, since to feel sorrow and pain is to be human. You can't control another person's acceptance of your apologies, but you can be willing to make amends and live in truth.

If harsh words meet your humility, resist the urge to defend or retaliate. Such moments are invitations to embody patience and grace. Remember, the pain of another often speaks louder than your apology can answer. Give space. Keep the door of your heart open without pushing them through it. Remain gentle, kind, and apologetic under fire, being aware of the pain of the other and the role you played in causing that pain. Your kind and repentant presence, even when offered in silence, can be more potent than words spoken in self-defense and out of your pain.

When the path to direct amends is blocked (by death, distance, or danger), God still makes a way for closure to occur. Pour your sorrow into an unsent letter, or let love flow into an act of service done in their honor. Healing can find you, even if reconciliation never does. I've often found that symbolic acts (such as writing a letter to the person, planting flowers or a tree, lighting a candle, or serving in an area of need) can become living memorials of your lament, repentance, and hope.[15] Redirect your energies in caring for those who've suffered similar wounds and losses, turning regret into redemptive service and compassion.

Your task is obedience, not outcome. Offer what's yours to give: truth, remorse, and the will to restore. Lay the result in God's hands, where justice and mercy meet. Trust that the One who sees in secret cherishes the courage it took to stand in the light unarmed. God hears our apologies, our laments, and our repentance, even when they're unanswered. The Spirit of Christ receives these as offerings of our hearts. Results can't measure faithfulness.

14. Sande, *Peacemaker.*

15. Alcoholics Anonymous, *Twelve Steps and Twelve Traditions*, 83–84.

Following Jesus is about having the courage to do the right thing even when it changes nothing visible.

## Making Restitution Where Possible

Restoration is more than repayment; it's a sacred act of truth-telling in deed.[16] When you return what was taken or repay what was lost, you declare that love now governs where selfishness once ruled. Each step toward restitution becomes a quiet hymn of justice. God makes all things new through divine grace and love, and when we engage in restitution, we partner in God's work, even if only in a small, fragile, humble way. When we seek to make some form of restitution, we're saying, "Your worth and dignity are greater than my past harm."

Words can soothe, but actions prove.[17] Restitution embodies repentance, revealing that the heart has turned toward righteousness. Even if the one wronged says it's unnecessary, the effort bears witness to inner transformation: a visible sign that grace has reshaped both intention and behavior. Trust is fragile, and people are often wary of words and promises (frequently rightly wary, given our past harms and broken promises). When we consistently follow through over time, we begin to build trust in ways that apologies or a single conversation cannot. When quietly and humbly repairing damage and acting with integrity without fanfare, we reveal that our hearts seek healing, truth, and change, not recognition.

Some wounds are beyond repair. Time can't be returned, nor can all sorrow be undone.[18] Yet the humility of doing what can be done speaks volumes. It confesses, "I can't heal everything, but I'll honor you with what's within my power to restore." It can help to admit what can't be fixed. Doing so shows maturity and respect, as well as a willingness to let go of control and release yourself and others from unrealistic expectations. Healing is God's work, so we can entrust what's beyond repair to the Spirit, knowing that God is at work in the world bringing life and new creation in ways we may never see.

When resources are scarce, creativity can redeem the gap. Acts of service, offering skills, or supporting a cause meaningful to the person can speak as loudly as any form of repayment. In love's economy, generosity of spirit often carries more weight than gold, planting seeds of reconciliation

16. Marshall, *Beyond Retribution.*

17. This is a paraphrase of the age-old proverb "Actions speak louder than words," rooted in centuries-old wisdom.

18. Tutu, *No Future Without Forgiveness.*

in hidden soil. Consider what matters most to the person you've harmed. Without fanfare or even telling them you're doing this, seek to contribute time and effort to those causes that matter to them, as a way of honoring and loving them and also those whom you'll serve, expressing your willingness to align your energy with their good, to show your repentance and change in practical ways, and to join with God as God restores the world to God's original good intent.

## Building Trust Over Time

Trust is a sacred thread; easily frayed, slowly rewoven.[19] In the aftermath of addiction or betrayal, it's common to long for instant restoration. But trust doesn't return through promises; it grows slowly through consistency. When a heart has been wounded, it watches not for apologies but for patterns.[20] Will you show up? Will your words match your actions? Will you remain sober, truthful, and patient when misunderstood? These are the bricks of restoration.

Expect some resistance. Loved ones may still flinch from old echoes. Their caution isn't cruelty; it's the memory of pain. Don't meet their hesitance with offense. Let it humble you. Let it call forth a deeper faithfulness.

Keep showing up. Keep living clean. Keep telling the truth when a lie would be easier. Pay attention. Be kind without needing to be seen. As you do, you plant seeds in soil scorched by disappointment. With time, they sprout.

This is slow work, but holy work. Over months and years, small acts of faithfulness (an honest word, a kept appointment, a gentle tone) stack up like stones to rebuild what was torn down. This isn't just damage control; it's the creation of something better. Relationships rebuilt on truth and humility often run deeper than before.

Remember this proverb: When we live in ways that align with divine goodness, even strained relationships can find rest. Not because we've forced them into harmony, but because peace has returned through our posture, our persistence, our surrender. Trust, once broken, becomes possible again: not by force, but by grace wrapped in time.

19. Prov 3:3–4.

20. Jas 2:18.

## Healing Relationships Through God's Grace

Forgiveness isn't engineered. Reconciliation isn't manufactured. These aren't human accomplishments, but gifts of grace. You may pray, reach out, and apologize with sincerity, yet still find silence. Or defensiveness. Or rejection. And yet, the work of healing in relationships belongs not first to us, but to the mercy of God.

Pray for those you've harmed. Speak their names in prayerful moments. Ask not only for their healing but also for your heart to be made spacious with compassion. Let grace soften you. The more you become like Christ, the more you carry the scent of peace, the possibility of redemption.

Sometimes, grace moves swiftly: A mother forgives with tears, a friend embraces you after years of silence. Other times, grace is slow, working beneath the surface, hidden like roots in winter. You may not see it yet, but something is moving. Trust that the Spirit is at work in places you cannot reach.

And if complete reconciliation never comes? Keep living a life that makes peace possible. Let your presence become an offering. In time, some may return. Others may not. But your journey isn't wasted. Even if reconciliation is partial or distant, your posture of humility leaves the door open.

In this way, your healing becomes a conduit for others. You who once broke trust can become the one who models restoration. The wound you inflicted may become the place where divine mercy overflows, not erasing the past but transforming it into testimony.

Recovery isn't just for you. It's for your children, your community, your future. You may become a bridge across generations. Through you, estranged families may speak again. Through you, a legacy of addiction may give way to a lineage of peace.

Don't underestimate the reach of grace. Reconciliation is a miracle. But it's also a calling. Walk into it with hope.

## Forgiving Others' Responses

Forgiveness is never a one-way street. As you walk the hard road of making amends (offering an open heart, humble and honest words, and an exposed and vulnerable soul), you may meet resistance, not embrace. Often, that's understandable, given people's pain from the past. A parent might lash out. A friend might rehearse every past wound. A child may reject your efforts to connect with them. Some may twist your confession into condemnation. And there, in the very moment you seek grace, you'll need to give it.

This is the deeper work: forgiving not just what has been done to you in the past, but what unfolds in the fragile now. To forgive someone's harsh response while you're offering peace is to embody the mercy you long to receive. It's turning your pain into prayer, your disappointment into a humble resolve not to retaliate. It's understanding that some hearts are still healing, some still bleeding, and their reaction may speak more of their wounds than your worth.

Let grace run full circle. Extend it to the ones who can't yet accept your apology, to those whose fear comes out sideways, to the voices shaped not by tenderness but by unresolved grief or anger. Forgiving their response doesn't mean condoning cruelty; it means you refuse to let bitterness retake root, not even in this sacred act of repentance.

You aren't responsible for how others carry their pain. You're responsible for your integrity, your humility, your honesty, your desire for reconciliation, your willingness to respect people's reactions and feelings, your ability to let people go if they ask for that, and your choice to show up with truth and love. And if your outstretched hand is met with silence, or resistance, or blame, that doesn't nullify your courage: it magnifies it. You've chosen the narrow path, the honest way, the Jesus-shaped road. That choice matters.

Forgiveness frees both ways. As you forgive the responses that sting, you guard your soul against fresh resentment. You keep your heart soft, your conscience clean, your recovery anchored in grace. Not every wound will be healed today. Not every relationship will be restored. But you can walk forward unshackled, knowing you've done what's yours to do.

This is no small thing. This is kingdom work. This is the weight and wonder of reconciliation. And whether others receive it or not, you're free, because you've chosen the way of peace, even when peace isn't returned.

Let this moment rest in you (the turning of your heart toward repair), trusting that even the smallest act of grace can ripple further than you'll ever see.

## Reflection Questions

1. Where have I most clearly experienced God's grace in my relationships during my recovery journey?
2. What fears or hesitations do I still carry about making amends, and how might I offer these to God in prayer?

3. When I think about the people I've hurt, what practical ways can I show humility and sincerity as I seek reconciliation?
4. How does Jesus's example of grace and forgiveness shape the way I respond to those who may not yet be ready to forgive me?
5. In what ways might I need to forgive myself so I can offer fuller love and presence to others?

## Action Steps

1. Spend time this week praying specifically for one person you've hurt, asking God to prepare both your heart and theirs for reconciliation.
2. Identify one practical way you can demonstrate your change to someone close to you: through honesty, service, or a kept commitment.
3. Read Luke 19:1–10 (Zacchaeus) and reflect on what tangible "restitution" might look like in your own life today.
4. If you can't yet make direct amends, choose a symbolic act of kindness or service that honors the person or repairs similar harm.

# 7.

# Growing in Christ

## New Habits and Holy Living

BEFORE WE FORM NEW habits, we must first imagine a new life. Recovery isn't merely about what we leave behind, but what we now embrace: daily rhythms of grace, holiness, and presence. Healing must become expressed in habits and mercy in motion.

### Establishing Daily Surrender

As part of my recovery from alcoholism, I've tried to spend time each day recommitting myself to Christ and surrendering to him. Surrender isn't a single moment; it's a rhythm, a returning, and a daily posture of the soul. It's the daily recalibration of a heart that knows its need. In the morning stillness, before the noise of the world can flood in, we say prayers, not of triumph but of trust: "Here I am again, God. I can't do this on my own. Hold me steady. Please help me in my weakness and need. Give me the strength only you can provide."[1]

Recovery flourishes not in self-reliance but in repeated surrender. One day at a time. One breath at a time. One choice to depend on Christ's Spirit at a time.[2] We don't graduate from our dependence; we grow deeper into it. The danger isn't relapse alone, but the creeping pride that says, "I've got this now." That lie is subtle, seductive, and always nearby. But daily surrender

1. Alcoholics Anonymous, *Alcoholics Anonymous*, 83–88.
2. Alcoholics Anonymous, *Alcoholics Anonymous*, 86.

interrupts it with truth. Each morning is an altar. Each waking moment is an invitation to yield.

This isn't weakness; it's wisdom. Those who walk in humility are the ones who rise with strength. To entrust your will and life to God each day isn't a fallback; it's a foundation.[3] Christ showed us that their power lies in vulnerability, strength in dependence, and grace in trusting God and God's divine empowerment and will. Humility and surrender steady you when temptations arise, when emotions surge, and when old patterns claw at the door. Surrender centers you in grace before the battle even begins.

Create a rhythm. Light a candle. Kneel beside the bed. Say the prayer. Write it on a sticky note. Let your body, your spirit, and your space remember: This life is no longer mine to run alone. Recovery is a partnership: your honesty and God's help, your courage and God's compassion, and your weakness and God's power. For me, it's a daily time of sitting with my Bible after breakfast, inviting God to strengthen and guide me throughout the day.

This habit, simple as it may seem, is a profound act of rebellion against the illusion of control. In a world obsessed with independence, surrender is a sacred form of resistance.[4] It marks you as one who belongs to something greater. It guards your sobriety not with fear but with freedom, not with gritted teeth but with open hands.

Begin again today. And tomorrow. And the next. One surrendered morning at a time, you'll find yourself walking paths you thought were closed, experiencing joy where despair once lived, and resting in the quiet strength of a grace that meets you fresh with the dawn. This is how transformation unfolds, not in grand gestures but in the daily "yes."

## The Power of Prayer and Meditation

Prayer and meditation can be the heartbeat of recovery for many people.[5] These spiritual practices draw the soul from the frantic noise of compulsion into the still waters where healing begins and the soul learns to surrender to God's love, presence, and enabling.[6] In addiction, the mind becomes a storm: memories, cravings, regrets, and fears colliding in restless motion. Prayer steadies that storm. Meditation anchors the heart in presence, creating space where we can receive God's grace, learn to follow Jesus as a disciple, and trust in the nearness and power of the Holy Spirit.

3. Alcoholics Anonymous, *Alcoholics Anonymous*, 59–60.
4. Rohr, *Breathing Under Water*.
5. Alcoholics Anonymous, *Alcoholics Anonymous*, 85–88.
6. Ps 46:10; Matt 11:28–29.

Prayer isn't merely speaking words into the air.[7] Prayer is opening the inner room to the One who already knows our wounds, our failures, and our longing for freedom. In prayer, we step away from self-reliance and dare to trust divine strength. It becomes a daily surrender, a humble confession that we can't save ourselves but can be remade, and a sacred source of hope and God's unconditional, ever-present love.[8]

Meditation deepens this surrender.[9] Meditation isn't emptying the mind into a void but filling it with the reality of God's nearness and the words of the Bible. As we slow our breathing, attend to Scripture, or rest in silence, the noise of shame and fear is quieted. Over time, these moments of stillness reshape us, softening hard places and awakening gratitude, guiding us toward self-awareness, compassion, love, and wisdom.

For those in recovery, prayer and meditation become both a shield and a compass. In moments of temptation, they provide refuge. In seasons of confusion, they offer clarity. They don't remove the struggle, but they remind us we aren't alone in it. They form a sacred rhythm (morning and evening, in solitude and community, in good times and bad) that keeps the soul aligned with what is true and life-giving.

This rhythm will feel awkward at first, especially for those unaccustomed to stillness. The mind will wander, the words may stumble. But over time, persistence turns these faltering beginnings into deep wells of strength. Even short, honest prayers ("Help me," "Thank you," "Stay with me") can hold the power to shift the day's trajectory.

Prayer and meditation do more than comfort; they transform. They dismantle the old scripts of despair and write new ones shaped by hope. They're a daily meeting point between weakness and mercy, between longing and fulfillment. And in that meeting, something holy happens: the recovering heart learns to rest, listen, and trust.

In this stillness, the soul hears again: You are loved, you are held, you are free.

## Feeding on Scripture Daily

Scripture is bread for the soul, and in recovery, the soul is often starving. Addiction drains the spirit, leaving it malnourished, thin, and restless. The promises of God aren't luxury food for the strong; they're daily sustenance for the weary. Each word is seed, light, and living water, speaking life into

7. Matt 6:6.

8. 2 Cor 5:17. See Foster, *Celebration of Discipline*; and Willard, *Hearing God*.

9. Ps 1:2–3; Josh 1:8.

places that once felt beyond repair. Scripture nourishes us, guides us, encourages us, convicts us, shapes us, changes us, leads us to repentance, and fills us with hope.

To feed on Scripture is to refuse the empty calories of lies, escapism, and despair. It's choosing truth over the counterfeit narratives that addiction once told: "You can't change. You're too far gone. This is who you'll always be. You need this substance or behavior to cope. You're hopeless and a failure." In the pages of Scripture, those lies meet the voice of God that says, "You are new. You are loved. You are held. You are precious. You can change. You are mine."

Reading daily isn't about checking a religious box but about returning, again and again, to the source. Like manna in the wilderness, the nourishment comes one day at a time.[10] Yesterday's reading won't meet today's hunger. The heart must be fed afresh, letting the Spirit speak into today's battles, today's choices, today's hope.

This daily reading and reflection on the Bible isn't always easy. There will be mornings when the mind feels foggy, when the words seem dry on the tongue. But persistence matters. Over time, habits shape the heart. Verses begin to surface unbidden during moments of temptation. Stories of redemption become mirrors, showing that the God who delivered then still delivers now.

For those rebuilding trust (with others, with themselves), Scripture becomes a tutor in truthfulness. It reveals the God who keeps promises and calls us to do the same. For those wrestling with shame, it unveils mercy that runs deeper than failure.[11] For those tempted to despair, it tells of a love that endures through every wilderness.

Let the reading be slow. Linger on a phrase. Pray it back. Journal what it stirs. Memorize a line and carry it with you throughout the day as a symbol of grace. This isn't about speed but saturation: allowing the word to soak into thought, memory, and action until it becomes part of the soul's vocabulary.

In recovery, feeding on Scripture daily isn't optional fuel; it's life itself.[12] For here, in these living words, the broken are nourished, the weary are strengthened, and the lost are found again.

10. Exod 16:4–5.

11. Lam 3:22–23.

12. Deut 8:3; Matt 4:4.

## The Habit of Worship and Gratitude

Gratitude is a posture that reorients the heart. Praise and worship are its voice.[13] Together, worship and gratitude form a rhythm strong enough to steady the soul through storm and temptation. Addiction often trains the body to notice only what's missing, what's broken, what's immediate, what's carnal, and what's craved. Worship and thanksgiving undo that pattern. They draw the eye away from emptiness and fix it on the abundance of grace already given in Christ Jesus our Lord.[14]

Practicing gratitude isn't about denying pain. It's to insist that pain isn't the whole or final story. Every breath, every sunrise, every flower, every smile, every meaningful relationship, and every act of kindness testifies that life is still a gift. In naming these gifts aloud, even the smallest ones, we anchor ourselves in the truth that goodness isn't absent. Gratitude shifts the gaze from what has been lost to what's being renewed. Just as marriages and relationships built on gratitude usually endure and deepen, so too does Christian discipleship and spirituality built on gratitude foster resilience, character, and depth.

Worship builds upon this gratitude by directing it heavenward. When we sing, pray, gaze at creation, sit in silent adoration, or lift our voices in words of praise, we step outside the echo chamber of self and enter a larger story. Worship reminds us that God isn't only the source of our healing but the center of all creation's song.[15] In worship, we remember we aren't alone. Our voices join with saints and angels (heavenly and worldwide), and with all that lives and breathes.

This habit isn't about waiting until we feel thankful. It's about choosing to give thanks amid struggle. In pain, struggle, persecution, anxiety, joy, hope, success, and even times of misstep, we give thanks to God for God's character, love, and sustenance, knowing all things will be made whole and right in Christ.[16] Gratitude is most transformative when it costs us something, when it arises from a heart still aching, still fighting, yet daring to believe that love is greater than despair. Worship in such moments becomes prophetic: a declaration that grace is real, that God is on the throne, that Christ has won the victory, that my mind and body will be restored in Christ's work on the cross, even when shadows whisper otherwise.

13. 1 Thess 5:16–18.
14. Phil 4:6–7; Col 3:16–17.
15. Rev 4:11; Ps 148.
16. Jas 1:2–4; Phil 1:29.

Practically, this means cultivating simple rituals. Keep a journal of gratitude, writing down three things each day, no matter how small. Begin prayers not with requests but with thanks. Sing even when your voice cracks. Light a candle as a symbol of hope and offer praise into the silence. These practices may seem small, but repeated daily, they carve pathways of joy into the mind and soul.

My mother has the habit of writing a list at the end of each year of the things that happened in her life during that year and giving thanks. This practice keeps her focused on God's presence in her life and fills her with gratitude. She has inspired my wife and me to do the same.

Over time, worship and gratitude reshape recovery.[17] They remind us we're more than our failures, more than our cravings, more than our wounds. They root us in a reality where mercy is new every morning. To live in gratitude and worship is to live free: not free of struggle, but free in spirit, unchained by bitterness, alive to grace.

## Fellowship and Church Involvement

Recovery is never meant to be a solitary path. It's often said that just as a coal pulled from the fire soon grows cold, so the soul left alone too long can lose its warmth and strength.[18] Fellowship rekindles what isolation weakens. In the gathering of believers (imperfect, broken, stumbling, yet carried by grace), we find both shelter and sharpening. It's also often said that the church isn't a club for the flawless but a hospital for the wounded, where stories of failure meet songs of redemption, and where weary travelers learn to walk again.[19]

It's tempting to airbrush away the flaws of the church, to form an image of the church in our minds, hearts, and rhetoric that's so perfect and flawless it resembles some strange, otherworldly, too-perfect image created by AI. But no community is like that. The church is a community of people who come together in all their messiness, brokenness, neediness, egocentricities, selfishness, and pain, and in all their beauty, love, hope, and many reflections of the image of God. The church is a complex picture, just as you and I are complex, and the church deserves our grace and hope, just as we need the same. Among this ragtag group of people we pilgrim together in

17. Voskamp, *One Thousand Gifts*; Foster, *Celebration of Discipline.*

18. This is a proverbial saying commonly attributed in Methodist circles to John Wesley, and used in early revival preaching. Wesley, *Journal of John Wesley.*

19. This saying was popularized in modern form by Yancey, *What's So Amazing About Grace?*

confession, vulnerability, honesty, and recovery, knowing that God makes all things new, and forms us into a new creation.

To step into fellowship is to risk vulnerability. It's to be known not just for triumphs but for wounds and scars. Yet this risk holds the seed of healing. When we confess struggles in community, shame loses its grip. When we worship side by side, voices blend into a chorus that reminds us we aren't alone. Even the smallest acts (sharing a meal, tending gardens, praying together, serving shoulder to shoulder) become sacraments of belonging.

Addiction isolates. It breeds secrecy, mistrust, and fear. The church, at its best, stands as the opposite: a place where light exposes lies, where accountability is shaped by love, and where grace invites us to keep moving forward even when we stumble. Community doesn't erase struggle, but it bears it together, making the load lighter.

Scripture teaches that we're members of one body, each part needing the other.[20] Recovery thrives when surrounded by this living body of Christ. Here, encouragement strengthens resolve, wise counsel offers direction, and forgiveness creates space for new beginnings. Even in conflict or misunderstanding, there lies an opportunity to practice patience, mercy, and reconciliation: the very skills recovery demands.

Fellowship also calls us outward. It's not only about what we receive but about what we give. Serving in the church (whether in unseen acts of hospitality or public acts of ministry) reminds us that our lives matter, that our hands and hearts can bless others. Purpose is rediscovered when love is poured out, not hoarded.

So plant yourself in a community, however imperfect. See the best in fellow pilgrims. Show up. Pray with others. Share your story when the Spirit gives courage. Sing loudly. Serve faithfully. Love unconditionally. Forgive liberally. Use your gifts. See yourself as part of a community that includes you, but is bigger than you. In these rhythms, the Spirit forms resilience and hope. Fellowship becomes not just an aid to recovery but a foretaste of the kingdom of God, where broken lives are bound together in love, and grace is the bond that holds all things.[21]

## Serving and Giving Back

As I approach sixty, I can testify that the most joyous and meaningful times of my life have involved serving others. I also found in my recovery from alcohol addiction that serving in my church and neighborhood helped me

20. 1 Cor 12:12–27; Rom 12:4–5.

21. Bonhoeffer, *Life Together.*

lift my eyes from my struggles and focus on the needs of others. I'm sure I'm not the only person to feel that my soul is never more alive than when I pour myself out for another.

Recovery isn't only about being healed but about becoming a channel of healing for others. Henri Nouwen talks about being a "wounded healer."[22] At first, this seems impossible. A person who's been rescued from the edge may feel too fragile, too unfinished, too unworthy to give. Yet this is precisely where the miracle of grace shines. Out of broken vessels flow living streams.[23] Out of the wounded comes compassion. Out of scars comes testimony.[24]

You and I won't ever arrive at some distant perfection, so we don't serve when we reach some unattainable state. Instead, we offer what we have, even while we're still learning to walk again, believe again, feel freedom again. Volunteering at church, helping stack chairs after a recovery meeting, making coffee for others, or simply being present with someone who's hurting: these small acts matter. Faithful acts of service turn your gaze outward, loosening the grip of self-absorption and despair. The paradox of service is that in giving to others, you find your heart healed in ways you never expected.

Those who walk this path discover a profound truth: helping others is one of the surest ways of helping yourself. As Henri Nouwen observed, we follow the way of Jesus, healing our wounds while actively healing the wounds of others. Encouraging a newcomer to take their first steps toward sobriety strengthens your own. Sharing how you stumbled and stood up again builds resilience in both listener and speaker. Service nurtures dignity, reminding you that your life isn't wasted, that even the mess of your past can be repurposed into light for someone else's darkness.

I'm not merely proposing good psychology; service is the shape of the gospel itself, an expression of the love Christ modeled and called us to live out as his disciples. The one who came not to be served but to serve showed us that the way up is always the way down.[25] Service isn't weakness; it's a potent expression of love and vulnerability, and of power made holy. When you serve, you align yourself with the heart of Christ. Recovery deepens as you learn that your story isn't only about you. It's about joining the great work of redemption, one cup of cold water at a time. Start small.

22. Nouwen, *Wounded Healer.*

23. 2 Cor 4:7.

24. Nouwen, *Wounded Healer.*

25. Mark 10:45.

Stay faithful. And let service become the soil where purpose, joy, sobriety, love, freedom, and discipleship put down deep roots.

## Guarding Your Heart and Mind

Every recovery journey eventually faces this sobering reality: What you allow into your heart and mind will shape you. Sobriety isn't sustained by willpower alone but by cultivating a sanctuary within. The eyes and ears are gates; what passes through them either nourishes or corrodes the soul. If addiction once filled those gates with images of despair, substances of escape, or voices of shame, now wisdom calls you to guard them with care.

This is one of the reasons I took six months off most social media in 2025. Social media had become an unhealthy environment for me, filled with too many things that sparked envy, anger, or frustration in me. Guarding my heart and mind meant taking some time out.

Choosing to step away from things that tempt our hearts or pollute our minds isn't about legalism or fear but about holy discernment. The apostle Paul urged us to think on what is true, noble, lovely, and pure.[26] That wisdom remains a compass today. It might mean turning off streaming or television shows that glorify the very substances that once enslaved you. It might mean limiting the endless scroll of social media, where comparison, self-promotion, and distraction poison the spirit and mind. It might even mean stepping away from specific conversations or friendships that continually pull you back into old patterns. Guarding your heart is about asking the vital, piercing question: Does this bring me closer to the life God intends, or does it draw me away from it?

Boundaries are essential here. Some relationships will need to be held at a distance, not in bitterness but in clarity. Certain activities (overwork, overstimulation, doom scrolling, unrestrained indulgence) must be checked before they spiral into new forms of bondage. Recovery isn't only about what you stop but also about what you start. Fill the mind with Scripture, with music that lifts rather than depletes, and with voices that remind you of hope and dignity. Read books, walk through nature, join a group serving your community, attend worship services, plant a garden, befriend your neighbors, learn a musical instrument, or do something else that enriches your heart. Invite into your space what strengthens your spirit rather than weakens it.

26. Phil 4:8.

This practice requires vigilance, but it also cultivates peace. As you guard your heart, you begin to notice a new resolve within.[27] The noise lessens. The cravings lose power. Temptations that once seemed overwhelming are met with resilience born of intentional choices. Guarding your heart is less about building walls and more about planting gardens. You're choosing the soil in which your thoughts and desires will grow.

Over time, this discipline bears fruit. Sobriety is about what we preserve and strengthen. The mind becomes a place where the Spirit's voice can be heard more clearly. The heart becomes less cluttered, more spacious for love, truth, hope, faith, and joy. In guarding what comes in, you protect the miracle of recovery and nurture the life God is growing within you.

## Healthy Body, Healthy Life

A significant part of my recovery involved choosing to engage in daily exercise, primarily walking with my dog every day. Recently, my wife and I have joined the gym. I'm aware that as I grow older, I need to protect my body through resistance training. Staying healthy and continuing in recovery go hand in hand in my life.

The body tells the truth even when the mouth stays silent. Weariness shows in the eyes, stress lingers in the shoulders, hunger aches in the bones. Recovery isn't just a spiritual or mental endeavor; it's embodied. We're whole beings, knit together in ways that can't be divided. When the body is neglected, the spirit suffers. When the body is cared for, the soul has space to breathe.

Addiction often left the body depleted: sleep disrupted, nutrition ignored, mind undernourished, and strength diminished. The journey back requires gentleness with oneself, a willingness to see self-care not as indulgence but as holy stewardship. A walk in the morning air, the steady rhythm of lungs filling and emptying, can become a prayer without words. A whole night's rest is more than just recovery; it's about trust, laying down control, and letting the body restore itself. Healthy food, prepared and savored, isn't just fuel but thanksgiving, a way of saying, "this body matters; this life's worth tending."

The Scriptures remind us that our bodies are temples, dwelling places of the Spirit.[28] To care for the body is to honor the presence of God within.[29] Exercise, sleep, and nourishment are not distractions from the spiri-

27. Prov 4:23.

28. 1 Cor 6:19–20.

29. Rom 12:1.

tual life but expressions of it. Even something as simple as deep breathing during a moment of craving can be a form of prayer. Inhale grace, exhale fear. Inhale peace, exhale despair. These embodied practices ground the soul, reminding us that recovery isn't abstract; it happens in flesh and blood, in muscle and breath.

Caring for the body also protects against relapse. Exhaustion and stress weaken resistance, making old temptations whisper louder. By tending to physical health, you build a shield around your heart and mind. Physical care isn't vanity, but vigilance; not selfishness, but stewardship. Each act of care (choosing rest, drinking water, moving the body) becomes a small "yes" to life, a declaration that the gift of this body will no longer be squandered but cherished.

Treating the body kindly is an act of gratitude. It says, "I believe this life is being restored, and I'll honor it." In recovery, healthy habits aren't separate from spiritual habits; they're interwoven, each supporting the other, forming a life where wholeness can flourish.

## Learning Continually

When I stopped drinking alcohol in 2025, I knew I needed to nourish my mind, replacing old habits with new ones. I enrolled in a Doctor of Philosophy program at Flinders University in South Australia, and the learning process was beneficial for my heart and recovery.

The soul shrivels when it ceases to grow. Stagnation is fertile soil for relapse; boredom and complacency can undo what months of sobriety have built. To recover is to awaken to a life of possibility, where learning isn't a duty but a doorway. Growth keeps hope alive. Curiosity fuels resilience. A life set in motion refuses to drift back into the shadows.

Learning can take many forms. It may be diving deeper into Scripture, not just reading but studying, wrestling, and letting the ancient words shape new understanding. It may involve attending a workshop, joining a retreat, attending a conference, enrolling in a course, or reading a book on recovery or spiritual formation. It may even be pursuing job skills or education, discovering talents and capacities that addiction once buried. Every new lesson learned is a brick laid in the foundation of a renewed life.

This pursuit isn't about collecting knowledge for its own sake, but about transformation. To learn continually is to confess that God always has more to reveal, that no one has arrived, and that each step forward is part of the unfolding. In recovery, learning teaches not only how to avoid old traps but how to embrace new callings. Through counseling, step work, or honest conversations, you gain greater clarity in understanding yourself, and in knowing yourself, you open up more fully to knowing God.

The act of learning itself becomes a spiritual discipline. It trains the mind to stay alert, the heart to remain humble, the spirit to keep open. It says, "I'm still becoming, still unfolding, still leaning toward the light." This posture of growth protects against the lie that recovery is merely about stopping a behavior. Recovery is about embracing a whole new life, filled with potential, purpose, and wonder.

There's joy here. The more you learn, the more expansive life becomes. Doors open. Perspectives shift. Courage grows. Thoughts expand. Hearts enlarge. A curious mind and a teachable heart are less likely to sink back into despair because they are continually being fed with vision for the future. Learning keeps you awake to the mystery of God's work in and around you.

To live in recovery is to live as a student of grace.[30] Every day holds something to be discovered. Every lesson, whether through Scripture, creation, or community, is a reminder: the story isn't finished.[31] You're still becoming, and God is still revealing.

## Perseverance in Trials

Storms will come. Recovery doesn't insulate anyone from the winds of grief, disappointment, or temptation. Since I've stopped drinking alcohol, I've experienced job losses, heartaches, relationship breakdowns, illness, bereavement, and more. Being sober hasn't protected me from pain, grief, sorrow, mistakes, and loss. Faith in Christ isn't an escape hatch from suffering but a way to walk through it without losing heart. Perseverance and character aren't forged in calm waters; the fire of trials shapes them when resolve is tested and dependence on grace deepens.

James spoke of trials as gifts in disguise, pressing us into patience and maturity. "Consider it pure joy, my brothers and sisters, whenever you face trials of many kinds, because you know that the testing of your faith produces perseverance. Let perseverance finish its work so that you may be mature and complete, not lacking anything."[32] What feels like resistance becomes the very weight that strengthens muscle. Each hardship carries within it an invitation: Will you collapse under the burden, or lean into the

30. 2 Pet 3:18.

31. Ps 19:1; 2 Tim 3:16.

32. Jas 1:2–4.

God who carries with you? In the end, perseverance is less about gritting teeth and more about learning to trust when everything shakes.

Recovery requires this vision. There will be days when cravings strike out of nowhere, when loss cuts deep, or when shame resurfaces. Don't interpret these as signs of failure but as reminders that you're still on the journey. Even if you stumble, God hasn't abandoned you. Scripture promises that "though the righteous fall seven times, they rise again."[33] Rising is the mark of the redeemed.

This is why perseverance matters: it transforms setbacks into stepping stones. Every time you choose to get back up, to turn again toward God, you declare that despair won't have the final word. You refuse to surrender to the old lies. You say with your life that grace is stronger than failure, that hope outlasts despair, that God is faithful in every valley.

Make it your resolve never to relinquish quitting your addiction, and to never give up on the possibility of transformation. Let perseverance be your companion, not as a cold command but as a living witness that you belong to the One who endured the cross and overcame.[34] Recovery isn't about perfection, but about persistence: a thousand daily choices to keep walking forward.

Hold fast. Trials will come, but they cannot undo what God has begun. Perseverance, born of grace, becomes not only your shield but your song: a testimony that no storm, however fierce, has the power to undo the work of love in you.

Pause here and breathe. Each step of surrender has carried you further into freedom, where grace is no longer an idea but the ground beneath your feet.

## Reflection Questions

1. Where in my life do I still feel tempted to give up when trials come, and how might God be inviting me to see these moments as opportunities for growth?
2. James speaks of perseverance leading to maturity. How have I already seen perseverance shaping my recovery journey?
3. When I stumble or feel weak, what does it mean for me to trust that God's grace is strong enough to help me rise again?

33. Prov 24:16.

34. Heb 12:2.

4. Who are the people or communities that I can rely on when life feels overwhelming, and how can I lean on them more fully?

## Action Steps

1. Begin each morning this week with a short prayer of perseverance. This prayer may be something as simple as, "God, help me stand firm today, whatever comes."
2. Write down one past trial that once felt unbearable but has now become a source of strength, and thank God for the growth that came through it.
3. Identify one person you can reach out to when you feel tempted to give up; send them a message or call them this week.
4. If a setback comes, practice getting up quickly: pause, pray, and take the next right step rather than dwelling in shame.

# 8.

# Fellowship and Purpose

## Thriving in Community and Calling

THE ROAD OF RECOVERY isn't only about turning away from what once enslaved us, but about stepping into the new life that grace and the way of Jesus make possible. Each day becomes a chance to choose again: to walk in light, to breathe in freedom, to rebuild broken relationships, and to trust that the God who began this work will see it through.

### No Longer Alone: The Importance of Fellowship

Addiction thrives in silence and solitude. It encourages us to abandon our support structures and friendships, to go it alone, and to make the addiction our only companion. Addiction speaks most loudly in the dark, convincing the wounded soul that no one could ever understand, that no one would ever care. Even in a crowded room, the ache of isolation can be crushing: a loneliness that feels deeper than words. But recovery tells a different story. It's the rediscovery that we were never meant to walk alone, that healing flows not only in prayer closets but also around kitchen tables, in recovery circles, and in sanctuaries where hearts are knit together by grace.

Scripture speaks with piercing clarity: "Two are better than one, because if one falls, the other can lift them up."[1] This is more than poetry; it's the practical wisdom of survival. In the trenches of recovery, you need people who'll notice when your shoulders sag, who'll ask hard questions,

1. Eccl 4:9–10.

and who'll celebrate even the smallest victories. Fellowship isn't an optional extra; it's the lifeline that keeps us tethered when the winds howl.

Most of us who have recovered from addiction know the experience of being tempted when we're tired, depressed, and lonely. Isolating ourselves from others only makes the experience worse. We also see the value of having others come alongside, encourage us, listen to our pain, and show solidarity with us in our shared humanity and our choice to be free of our addiction.

Jesus promised that wherever two or three gather in his name, he is there.[2] This means community isn't just mutual support; it's holy ground. God shaped us in the divine image, which means we're created for intimacy and communion with God and others. In the circle of believers, we experience the presence of Christ in ways that solitude can't replicate. God's Spirit dwells in the gathered body, binding wounds, bearing burdens, and teaching us to love beyond our capacity.

To step into fellowship is to renounce the lie that you must figure it out alone. It's about embracing vulnerability, about letting others see both your scars and your hope. In their prayers, you will hear echoes of God's compassion. In their forgiveness, you'll glimpse mercy. In their persistence, you'll feel the steady strength of grace.

You're no longer alone. Whatever shame told you in the night, whatever fear convinced you of abandonment, fellowship answers with truth: you belong, you're loved, you're precious, you can be free with the support of others and God. The church, the recovery group, and the small circle of trusted friends—these are the hands of God extended toward you. They won't always be perfect, but they will walk with you, and in their company, you'll discover again and again that Christ himself walks beside you.

## Finding Your Place in the Body of Christ

You fit in the larger family of faith. It took me a while to believe that was true, after my sense of remorse and regret from struggling with addiction, but God makes all things new, including you and me.

There's a deep hunger in every heart to belong. Addiction often strips that away, leaving a person feeling like an exile even in their skin. Many of us who come through addiction feel insignificant, alienated, or unloved. We need others who love and support us. Scripture paints a vision of a body where no part is unnecessary, no role forgotten, no scar disqualifying.[3]

2. Matt 18:20.

3. 1 Cor 12:12–27.

In this body, the wounded aren't discarded; they're welcomed as vessels through which grace shines more clearly.

The body of Christ isn't a gallery of perfect saints, but a living organism pulsing with diverse gifts.[4] One sings, another listens, one teaches, another serves quietly in the shadows. Each contribution is different, yet each is vital. Recovery makes this truth even sharper: The one who once staggered in shame can now stand as a witness of mercy; the one who knows the pit can speak life to others still reaching for the rope. What once was brokenness becomes a gift to the community, a reminder that resurrection isn't theory but reality.[5]

For those walking out of addiction, the lie often suggests, "You don't belong here. You're too tainted, too late, too small." Yet God's voice answers with steady assurance: "You're mine, and I've placed you here for a purpose." That purpose may not be evident at first. It may begin with stacking chairs, greeting at the door, listening to a friend in need, or showing up faithfully in a small group. But in those ordinary acts, a sense of belonging grows. Over time, unique gifts emerge: encouragement shaped by suffering, compassion sharpened by struggle, wisdom carved out of scars.

The invitation is simple yet profound: step into the body and take your place. Don't wait until you feel worthy; belonging isn't earned, it's given. You have a unique role to play in Jesus's body. You belong, and you have a unique, God-given, grace-filled contribution to make to God's people and the world. As you offer your gifts, however small, you'll discover that in Christ's body, you aren't just included, you're indispensable.[6]

## Accountability and Support Networks

Recovery can't thrive in secrecy. Healing flourishes when it's held in the light of trusted relationships. Accountability isn't about surveillance or control; it's about companionship on a road that is too rugged to walk alone.[7] In a world that prizes self-sufficiency, the gospel dares to say that weakness needs others, and that vulnerability is the seed of strength.

A support network is more than a circle of friends; it's a safety net woven from honesty, prayer, and mutual care. It's made of people who will notice the subtle signs: the missed meetings, the tired eyes, the silence that feels heavier than usual. These companions aren't there to condemn but to

4. Rom 12:4–8.
5. Rom 6:4; 2 Cor 5:17.
6. 1 Cor 12:22–26.
7. Gal 6:1–2; Bonhoeffer, *Life Together.*

remind you of who you are and what you've been called to. They're the ones you can call at midnight when cravings claw, the ones who will pray you through the storm and hold you steady until morning.

Practical wisdom helps here. Choose a few key people who can walk closely with you: an accountability partner, a mentor, a sponsor, and a mature believer whose life reflects faithfulness. Invite them into your real story, not the polished version.[8] Let them see the places where relapse feels near, where shame whispers loud, where the fight feels too much. Their presence creates a holy guardrail, keeping you from sliding into old ruts unnoticed.

Throughout my recovery, I've relied on close friends, mentors, family, psychologists, and spiritual directors to keep me accountable, asking the tough questions in love. There's no way I would have recovered without these people, and there's no way you'll recover and stay sober or free unless you have such people in your life. These people are the presence of God for us. You and I need them more than we'll ever realize. When we ask God to be close, they're there. When we ask Christ to support us, they're present. When we ask the Spirit to empower us, they're a helping hand. We all need accountability and support networks, and especially in recovery.

Inviting people into your life to support you isn't a sign of weakness; it's a sign of wisdom. Just as soldiers never stand watch alone, so those in recovery are strongest when they share the load. Scripture reminds us that two are better than one, for when one falls, the other lifts them up.[9] So let others have your back, and offer your strength in return. In such networks of grace, sobriety becomes more than survival; it becomes a shared testimony of God's sustaining power.

## From Isolation to Involvement

Addiction feeds in the dark corners of loneliness. Even in a crowd, the heart can feel abandoned, unseen, and unwanted. Yet the Spirit beckons toward light. To break isolation is to defy shame's whispers and step into fellowship, where presence itself becomes medicine, and love begins its quiet work. Reflect on when you've felt the pull to withdraw from others in your recovery journey, why you withdrew, and how the pull of isolation was deceiving you. Consider the people that God wants you to reach out to for support, instead of retreating into solitude.

Healing seldom comes through grand gestures; it begins with a shared cup of coffee, a laugh, or a hesitant "yes." Each choice to engage is an act of

8. Alcoholics Anonymous, *Alcoholics Anonymous.*

9. Eccl 4:9–10.

courage, a seed of belonging. These small steps accumulate, gently retraining the soul to believe that community is safer than solitude's false shelter. What's the small, practical thing you can do this week to move toward connection with others, such as making a phone call, having a coffee with someone, or joining a group gathering? These things may seem small, but they build trust, connection, and a sense of belonging over time.

When we open our lives to others, something sacred happens. Their stories mingle with ours, joy multiplies, burdens divide. The Spirit breathes through companionship, reminding us that love was never meant to be hoarded. Healing often hides in shared meals, vulnerable conversations, and the holy ordinariness of walking together. You may recall times when love, joy, healing, and freedom flowed through shared life with others, often through simple, everyday activities. During recovery, we need to honestly face the places where we resist letting others into our hearts and open ourselves to what the Spirit of Christ wants to do within us.

The community of faith does more than support; it transforms. What once held the soul captive loosens its grip when others stand beside us. Over time, the false promises of addiction lose power, replaced by friendships that steady trembling hands and voices that reassure, "You aren't alone anymore." Relationships help us resist the pull of addiction. We can learn to lean on others for strength, empathy, and accountability, allowing their support to build our confidence, guide our ways, and steady our steps.

## Discovering Your God-Given Purpose

From the beginning, every life was spoken into being with purpose.[10] We aren't accidents or afterthoughts but carriers of divine intention. Recovery clears the fog, making space to rediscover this truth. God has entrusted gifts within each of us, waiting to be awakened and offered for the sake of the kingdom. It may be hard to believe it, but God created you with divine intention and purpose, placing unique gifts within you that you can use to bless God's people and the world. You have experiences, gifts, and abilities within you that God can use for the sake of others' well-being, healing, and flourishing.

Addiction clouds vision, reducing life to cycles of craving and survival. Dreams dissolve into smoke, and the sense of calling becomes buried beneath shame. Yet loss isn't the final word. Even amid ruins, the Spirit whispers that purpose can be recovered, reshaped, and redeemed by grace's persistent hand. I've found it helpful in my recovery to name the ways

10. Palmer, *Let Your Life Speak*; Nouwen, *Life of the Beloved.*

addiction robbed me of confidence, purpose, passion, clarity, or direction. Then I ask God to help me let that fog go and, instead, to receive all the purpose and plans he has for me. You and I can trust that God can redeem lost years as the Spirit shapes us into a new creation, walking into the freedom and purpose Jesus has for our lives.

Recovery isn't only the ending of one story but the beginning of another. Here, new dreams are born: raising families in love, serving with compassion, and excelling in honest work. Purpose emerges when scars become testimonies, and wounds once hidden become the very places from which healing flows outward. Pause occasionally and recognize the signs of purpose beginning to emerge in your recovery journey. One of the most rewarding and freeing things we can do is allow our scars, struggles, and stories to become a source of encouragement, guidance, and healing for others. That's what I'm trying to do in this book, as I share my story.

Purpose unfolds best in prayerful surrender. Saying to Christ, "What do you desire to do through my life now that it's yours?," opens the heart to divine direction. This prayer awakens holy anticipation, reminding us that recovery isn't merely survival but a calling. God longs to shape each life into a larger handiwork of redemption. Praying simply, honestly, and with openness. Create space in your life to listen for God's leading about your calling and purpose. God is doing something remarkable in and through you, and as you open your heart to the Spirit's voice and leading, you may be surprised by the ways Jesus will shine through you and bless others.

## Turning Your Mess into a Message

The ashes of addiction may seem like a wasteland, but even in that broken soil, seeds of redemption can be sown. What once felt like shame beyond telling can become the testimony that unlocks doors for others still imprisoned. The Spirit doesn't waste wounds; every scar can become a signpost pointing toward mercy. Your pain, loss, learnings, and experiences can be a source of hope, warning, and guidance for others when you let the Spirit do God's work.

It's often in the places where life was most fractured that God chooses to work through us most powerfully. The comfort you have received in your darkest moments becomes a well from which others may drink. This isn't abstract hope; it's incarnate, lived, and embodied hope. Our changed hearts and lives testify to the God who makes people into new creations, through God's love and grace.[11] When you speak honestly of your struggle, someone else

11. 2 Cor 5:17.

sees themselves in your words and realizes they're not alone. What seemed like a valley of death becomes, in God's hands, a pasture of life for others.

This doesn't require a pulpit or microphone. It may be as simple as listening to someone's late-night fears without judgment, sitting with a newcomer at a recovery meeting, or sharing a gentle word with someone at church who looks weighed down by secrets. Your story, entrusted to you by grace, carries within it the power to break shame's silence. For me, it was sharing my story with a college class. For you, there will be another way God shares hope and grace, inspiring and encouraging others in their journey of freedom from addiction.

When you name where you've been and where God has met you, you remind yourself as much as anyone else that deliverance is real. God is the God who delivers people from bondage, and has been doing so since ancient times, continuing to do so to this day.[12] Telling your story becomes both a light for another's path and a shield for your recovery. It's harder to slip back into darkness when you're actively shining light into someone else's night.

So let your mess become your message, not in a way that glorifies the pain but in a way that magnifies the Deliverer. As you offer what you've learned and how you've been restored, you join the long line of witnesses whose lives declare that no pit is too bottomless for grace, and no past too tangled for redemption. The story of how God has met you in your mess, given you the grace and power to be free and find a new life, and the people and resources to maintain that freedom, can be a light to others and a testimony to the glory and goodness of our God. In this way, misery is transformed into ministry, and your scars become holy stories of hope.[13]

## Serving in the Church and Community

Freedom isn't only about leaving chains behind; it's also about learning to walk with hands open for others. One of the surest ways to remain anchored in recovery is to discover the joy of service: giving yourself away in love, just as Christ gave himself for the world. Jesus and the rest of the biblical narrative show us that serving others, expressing God's love, and giving yourself to the well-being and flourishing of humanity and creation is the way to fullness of life and freedom in God.

Perhaps during the years of addiction, gifts once treasured were set aside or forgotten. Music, art, teaching, caregiving, cooking, encouragement, or craftsmanship—all of these can be resurrected as instruments

12. Exod 3:7–10.

13. Nouwen, *Wounded Healer*.

of blessing. What was dormant can be reawakened by the Spirit, not only for your healing but for the flourishing of others. Service isn't limited to church programs; it's the daily practice of showing up with compassion and kindness. It might look like preparing meals for the homeless, mentoring a child, or simply offering a genuine welcome to someone walking through the church doors for the first time. Throughout your community and neighborhood, some people need support, connection, and love. If you open your heart and eyes, the Spirit will lead you to places where you can serve and enrich lives. We're told it's more blessed to give than to receive, and so many of us discover this when we give of our resources and hearts for others.[14]

When you serve, you are drawn out of self-preoccupation into the vast landscape of God's kingdom. This is why Jesus spoke so much about service, telling his disciples that service, humility, and love are at the heart of the kingdom of God. Addiction narrows vision until all that matters is the next fix or numbing escape. Service widens vision, calling you to see needs beyond your own and to discover the deep fulfillment of being the hands and feet of Christ.[15] In lifting burdens from others, you discover your own shoulders are lighter.

Serving also roots you in belonging. To take part in the life of a church or community is to claim your place as an active participant in God's kingdom, church, and mission. This is more than filling a role; it's learning to live as one who is indispensable to the body. Your presence and contribution matter. Each act of service testifies that you aren't only a survivor but a vessel of grace, called to pour out what's been poured into you.[16] The times in Christian life that have been most meaningful and memorable to me are times when I've served with others, and you'll discover the same.

And here lies the paradox of recovery: As you give, you receive. As you serve, you grow. When you give of yourself for the sake of others, serving with a loving and humble heart, you're imitating our Lord and Savior, Jesus Christ, who showed us what it means to serve, give, love, and be a vessel of God's goodness and grace.[17] The more you extend yourself in love, the less space there is for cravings, obsessions, or despair to take hold. Service keeps your heart outward-focused, your hands busy in compassion, and your spirit attuned to the movement of God in the world.

Step into the joy of serving. Let your gifts (whether simple or grand, hidden or obvious) be placed back into the flow of community. In doing so,

14. Acts 20:35.

15. Claiborne and Haw, *Jesus for President.*

16. 1 Pet 4:10.

17. John 13:12–15.

you will find that the life once stolen by addiction is now being multiplied, not just for you but for the blessing of many.

## Dreaming Again—Setting Goals

Addiction often steals the horizon. It narrows life until all you can see is the next craving, the subsequent escape, or the next collapse. Dreams are abandoned, goals forgotten, and the heart grows weary of hoping. But sobriety clears the fog, and faith roots us again in the soil of promise. Now, it's time to dream again.

These dreams aren't empty fantasies, but God-breathed possibilities. They're visions of healing, of wholeness, and of a future shaped not by addiction but by grace. Perhaps the Spirit stirs you to pursue education once dropped, to reconcile with a loved one estranged, to begin a venture that carries both risk and hope, or even to write the testimony that has been burning within you.

To dream in recovery is to declare that your story isn't finished. It's to trust that God has prepared good works for you to walk in, even after the ruins of the past.[18] These dreams, however, aren't to be grasped with clenched fists, but held with open hands: surrendered to the will of the One who knows you best. Plans are made, but steps are guided by God's steadying hand.

Set goals that are both small and grand: a short-term step that builds momentum, and a long-term vision that pulls you forward with hope. Each milestone reached, no matter how modest, becomes a stone of remembrance: a marker of God's restoring work. What was lost can be redeemed. What was broken can be made whole. What seemed impossible can blossom in season.

To dream in the Spirit is to resist the cynicism of this age. The world teaches us to dream in the language of control, visibility, and gain. But the dreams born of silence, prayer, and suffering are slow and subversive.[19] They don't seek applause; they seek faithfulness. They often begin in desert places, where ambition dies and the heart starts to listen again. The goals that emerge there aren't shaped by ego or urgency but by love, longing, and the ache for a world remade in mercy. To dream in Christ is to remember that we're dust and breath: fragile, limited, but held. And from that posture, we dare to imagine justice where there has been cruelty, community where there has been exile, and joy where there has been despair. These dreams

18. Eph 2:10.

19. Brueggemann, *Prophetic Imagination*.

are often costly and peculiar, too quiet for the marketplace and too tender for the algorithms. But they're the dreams that endure, because they're not about us; they're about the healing of the world.

Set goals that echo the gospel, not the world. Let them require community. Let them be interrupted by grace. Let them honor the least, disrupt the powers, and linger beyond your lifetime. True dreaming isn't a luxury for the privileged or a pastime for the restless: it's a holy discipline. It invites us to plant fig trees under falling skies, to begin where we are, to risk everything for a future that may never bear our name. These aren't goals to achieve, but callings to embody: measured not by success, but by surrender, not by outcomes, but by love. Jesus calls us to dream again: not with anxious striving, but with eyes fixed on resurrection, and hands open to the Spirit's surprising lead, for it is in dreaming (and in setting goals shaped by God's fierce, cruciform love) that we become participants in the redemption of all things.[20]

To dream again isn't to return to naïve ambition, but to live as one who knows that redemption has no expiration date. God's not done with you. Let your goals bear witness to that truth.

## Staying Connected and Giving Back

Recovery is never a solo journey, and neither is the life of faith. When the initial fire of freedom begins to feel familiar, a subtle temptation arises to drift: to loosen ties to fellowship, skip gatherings, and let old habits of isolation creep in. Yet the path of lasting transformation is one of deep connection and steady community.

Faith flourishes when it is shared. Commit yourself to rhythms of belonging: regular worship, honest conversations, and continued mentorship. Sometimes you'll need to be mentored, carried, and reminded of the truth when you grow weary. Other times, you'll be the one offering strength to another. Both giving and receiving are sacred, and both keep you rooted in the body of Christ.

Staying connected also cultivates gratitude. Recovery isn't just about what has been given to you, but about how that gift is multiplied in the lives of others. Grace received is never meant to be hoarded: it's meant to overflow. By offering your time, your talents, your presence, or even your simple kindness, you participate in the great exchange of grace that defines the kingdom.

Giving back protects your freedom. It reminds you that your life isn't only spared, but commissioned. You're no longer defined by what you took,

20. Moltmann, *Theology of Hope*; Wright, *Surprised by Hope*.

but by what you now give.[21] Whether it's volunteering at a ministry, mentoring a newcomer, or just being the one who shows up when someone needs help, you become a vessel of the same mercy that carried you through.

To give yourself to the church is to enter a mystery, not a machine. You join a people who break bread with the broken, hold silence with the suffering, and sing songs the world has forgotten how to hear. The church doesn't need your brilliance or strength; it needs your presence, your tears, your questions, and your prayers. And when you offer those freely, without demand or applause, you become part of the slow healing of all things. You're not giving back because of obligation. You're giving because grace has already undone you.

In a world that commodifies time and monetizes gifts, to give of yourself without return is a kind of holy foolishness.[22] But this is what the gospel invites. You hand over your time, your skills, your listening, and your laughter, not because they're flawless, but because they're yours to give. The offering of the self (half-broken, unfinished, uncertain) is the raw material of the kingdom. And when given into the hands of the crucified, it becomes Eucharist.[23] Not efficient. Not perfect. But blessed and multiplied in ways you may never see.

Freedom is sustained in this posture of connection and generosity. When recovery shifts from what you've escaped to what you contribute, joy deepens, humility grows, and gratitude anchors your soul. In staying connected and giving back, recovery becomes not just survival, but a living testimony of grace at work.[24]

## Living as a New Creation

There are many beautiful images in the Bible, and one of my favorites is the image of God as Creator who lovingly creates and sustains all things, invites us into co-creation with Christ and others, restores all creation at the end of the age, and makes us new creations in Christ Jesus.[25] We don't always feel like new creations, but God is recreating our bodies, hearts, minds, and spirits anyway, so that being made in God's image, we reflect his image in our entire beings and as we become like Christ.

21. Acts 20:35.

22. Hauerwas and Willimon, *Resident Aliens*; Cavanaugh, *Being Consumed.*

23. Schmemann, *For the Life of the World.*

24. Nouwen, *Wounded Healer.*

25. Gen 1:1; 2 Cor 5:17; Col 1:16–17; Rev 21:1–5; Wright, *Paul and the Faithfulness of God.*

To live as a new creation is to step into the dawn after a long night, to breathe air that once felt out of reach. Addiction chained your steps, silenced your song, and cast shadows over your identity. Yet in Christ, those chains have broken, and a new story has begun.[26]

The gospel proclaims that the old has passed away and the new has come.[27] This is the reality of resurrection made possible through the sacrifice, resurrection, and glorification of our Lord Jesus Christ. You're no longer identified by your failures or the labels the world has placed on you. "Addict," "broken," "lost": these are no longer your name. Your true name is beloved, child of God, disciple, friend of Christ, chosen, redeemed, holy, forgiven, light of the world, salt of the earth, heir with Christ, masterpiece, citizen of heaven, priest, saint, temple of the Spirit, and a new creation.[28] This new identity isn't earned by performance, productivity, or perfection, but received as a sheer gift.

Living as a new creation means putting on this new self each day. Like clothing yourself in garments of grace, you rise each morning and remember: I'm not who I was.[29] The shame doesn't define me. The past doesn't control me. I walk now in freedom, clothed in the righteousness of Christ.

This is flourishing in Christ, enabled by his grace, Spirit, and word. In community, you're no longer alone.[30] On mission, you're no longer aimless.[31] Your wounds, now healed, become testimonies of grace. Your presence becomes an offering of hope.

And though these pages draw to a close, your story doesn't. This is the beginning of a lifelong adventure with God, an unfolding journey of discovery, service, hope, love, faith, and joy.[32] Walk forward as a new creation, alive with purpose, sustained by grace, and radiant with the light of Christ. The old has gone. The new is here.[33] And the world needs the gift of your redeemed life.

Pause here, and let your soul rest in God's love. Chains once marked your life, but now God has clothed you in grace, called you beloved, and

26. See Volf, *Exclusion and Embrace*, on identity reshaped by reconciliation in Christ.

27. 2 Cor 5:17.

28. John 15:15; Rom 8:17; Eph 2:19; 1 Pet 2:9; 1 Cor 3:16; Matt 5:13–14.

29. Eph 4:22–24; Col 3:9–12.

30. Hays, *Moral Vision of the New Testament*, on the transformative identity of the Christian community.

31. Acts 2:42–47; Matt 28:19–20.

32. Phil 1:6; John 10:10.

33. 2 Cor 5:17.

empowered you for freedom and joy in the Holy Spirit. The life before you is nothing less than a new creation unfolding.

## Reflection Questions

1. Where in my recovery journey have I still felt the pull toward isolation, and how might God be inviting me into deeper community?
2. What unique gifts or experiences has God entrusted to me that could serve others in the body of Christ?
3. Who are the people I can lean on as my accountability network, and how might I also be a source of strength for them?
4. In what ways might God be transforming my pain or past failures into a message of hope for others?
5. How do I sense God stirring new dreams, goals, or purpose for this next season of my life?

## Action Steps

1. Choose one small step of connection this week: attend a group, share a meal, or reach out to someone you trust instead of staying isolated.
2. Prayerfully explore one area of service in your church or community where your gifts and story could bless others.
3. Identify one or two people who can serve as accountability partners and share your journey honestly with them.
4. Write down one dream or goal you sense God placing on your heart, and commit it to prayer, asking for guidance and next steps.

# Conclusion

## A Lifelong Journey of Growth and Dependence on God

Every journey of recovery is more than a struggle against chains. By God's lovingkindness, our recovery is the discovery of a deeper freedom, the kind only grace can bring. What began in brokenness now unfolds into a story of hope, a path marked by mercy, and a future alive with the promise of God's hope, freedom, and presence.[1]

### A Lifelong Journey of Growth

The road of recovery hasn't always been smooth or easy for me. There have been ups and downs, progress and setbacks, maturing and mistakes. Twenty years of sobriety have helped me understand that this is a lifelong journey of changing, resting in God's love, and growing to be the person God wants me to be.[2] You'll have the same experience, so don't give up.

The road of recovery doesn't end with the closing of a book. It stretches onward, winding through seasons of joy and hardship, lit by grace yet marked by the dust of daily struggle. To walk this path is to embrace a pilgrimage: never fully finished, constantly unfolding. Each step becomes both testimony and prayer, a reminder of how far you've come and how much further love can lead you.

Think of where the journey began: nights of despair, mornings of regret, a soul bound in chains that felt unbreakable. And now, through surrender, honesty, and mercy, you stand freer than before, carrying scars that no longer condemn but teach. This is no minor miracle. But it's also not

1. John 8:36; Rom 8:21.
2. Phil 1:6.

the finish line. Recovery and faith aren't trophies to be won once and for all; they're rivers to be entered daily, currents that call for trust and steady movement.[3]

Each day I say a prayer thanking God for divine grace and presence, for the ability to stay sober, for Christ's sacrifice on the cross, and for the Spirit's work in making me a new creation.[4] I know I'm carried by God, by Christian community, and by friends and family who love me.

There will be new lessons ahead, new temptations that test you, new callings that stretch you, and new depths of grace waiting to be discovered. To stay awake to this truth keeps you from drifting into complacency or pride. Humility teaches that healing is never complete this side of eternity, yet hope insists that growth never ceases either.

So let each dawn be welcomed as a gift and an invitation. Rise with gratitude for the ground already gained, but lean forward into the mystery of what God will yet do. One day at a time, one prayer at a time, one act of love at a time: you walk the lifelong road of growth. And in this ongoing journey, you discover that the One who began a good work in you is faithful, still guiding, still shaping, still bringing you into fullness.[5]

## Celebrate the Victory

There are moments in life that deserve to be named, honored, and savored. Recovery isn't simply surviving another day; it's resurrection, the rising of new life from places once buried in despair.[6] Take time to recognize what God has already done in you. You've stared into hard truths without flinching, released what once held you captive, and chosen paths that many never dare to walk. These choices, shaped by grace, mark a turning point that should be remembered with joy.

In August each year, I celebrate another year sober. That's twenty celebrations so far, as I thank God, friends, and family for the grace shown to me, and rejoice that Jesus has enabled me to stay on the path of sobriety. I find the annual celebration to be meaningful and memorable, and I look forward to it every year.

In one sense, this book you're holding is a celebration of my journey of recovery. Once I reached twenty years sober, rejoicing in August with loved ones that I'd enjoyed another year of freedom by God's grace and enabling,

3. Rohr, *Breathing Under Water*, 27–30.
4. Gal 2:20; 2 Cor 5:17.
5. Phil 1:6.
6. Rom 6:4; 2 Cor 5:17.

it struck me that I should write about my experience to help others. You don't need to wait twenty years, of course. Set regular milestones in your diary that are meaningful for you, and rejoice in the freedom and goodness of God. Over time, you'll develop your own ways of remembering where you've come from and celebrating God's work in your life. Recovery is hard, and it's worth reminding yourself of the incredible healing and freedom you're experiencing.

Celebration is a spiritual act.[7] When you pause to give thanks, you anchor your heart in gratitude, refusing to let the shadows have the last word.[8] Consider writing a letter to God, pouring out your thanks for the mercy you have received and the strength you have been given. Mark your milestones: a sobriety anniversary, a month of consistent prayer, the first time you shared your story openly. Invite loved ones into these moments so they, too, can witness the miracle of transformation. Their presence reminds you that recovery isn't only about your own healing, but also about the restoration of relationships and the ripples of hope that your life now carries.

Even if struggles remain, don't let them rob you of the victory you already hold. You're walking in freedom, however imperfectly, and that itself is worth rejoicing. Gratitude and joy do more than celebrate the past; they propel you forward. They remind you of the sweetness of freedom and fuel your desire to guard it. Every small victory is a down payment on the larger promise of wholeness that God continues to work in you. Lift your eyes, lift your heart, and let your spirit rejoice: you're alive, you're free, and you're walking in grace.

## Continue to Rely on God's Strength

As you look ahead, remember the truth that carried you here: it was never your strength alone. What has been born in you (the breaking of chains, the mending of your soul, and the healing of your mind and body) was the work of God's Spirit moving in hidden and powerful ways. The same power that raised Christ from the grave is the power that lifted you from the pit, and it won't abandon you now.[9]

Self-reliance offers promises of control, but it leads back into the same traps that once ensnared you. Guard your heart against that old temptation. Instead, stay rooted in the practices that connect you to divine strength. Begin your days with prayer, simple or profound. Feed your mind with

7. Dawn, *Royal Waste of Time.*

8. Phil 4:4–7.

9. Rom 8:11.

Scripture, letting its truth counteract the lies. Remain in fellowship, knowing that God's presence is often most deeply experienced through the love of others. Continue to see your mentor, sponsor, counselor, psychologist, and spiritual director, who invite their expertise to help you in your recovery and maintain your healing and freedom. Like a branch drawing life from the vine, your recovery depends on staying connected to the source of all strength and hope.[10]

Don't forget the promise: the One who began this good work in you will carry it to completion.[11] That means your story is still unfolding. There will be challenges ahead, but none greater than the grace that holds you. When temptation presses in, you aren't alone. When fear rises, you aren't forsaken. When joy fills your heart, you aren't forgotten. God is present, steady, and faithful.

Carry this truth into every step: you never fight alone. Your recovery isn't built on fragile willpower but on the unshakable strength of God's love. Lean into that strength daily, and it will hold you through every storm, guide you into deeper freedom, and carry you into the fullness of the life you were created to live.

## Your Life as a Light to Others

The story of your recovery isn't yours alone. Light is never meant to remain hidden under a basket; it is intended to pierce the darkness.[12] The healing you've tasted, the grace that has carried you, the forgiveness you've received, and the hope you've enjoyed are gifts for the world around you. Others stumble where you once stumbled, longing for a word of hope, a glimpse of freedom. Your scars, once signs of failure, now shine as proof that healing is possible and mercy is real.

Shining your light doesn't always mean standing on a stage or preaching to crowds. It might be as simple as showing kindness to the coworker who feels invisible, listening patiently to a friend in turmoil, or greeting a stranger with dignity. Sometimes light shines brightest in the quiet consistency of a life changed, where honesty replaces deceit, where patience replaces anger, and where love replaces indifference. In those daily choices, you reveal that freedom is possible, that addiction doesn't have the final word.

Still, there may also be moments when you're called into more intentional acts of service. You might walk alongside a newcomer in recovery,

10. John 15:4–5.
11. Phil 1:6.
12. Matt 5:14–16.

telling them, "I've been there, too, and you aren't alone." You might share your testimony in church or write your story for others who can't yet believe in their own redemption. The Great Commission doesn't belong only to preachers or teachers; it belongs to all disciples, including you.[13] Grace received becomes grace shared, and light given becomes light extended.

Never believe that perfection is required to serve. It's your honesty, not your polish, that others will find compelling. People connect not with the illusion of flawless strength but with the truth of a wounded heart made whole. Your willingness to tell the truth about your brokenness and the God who met you there becomes a lifeline for someone still drowning. Knowing your life carries this kind of weight and purpose isn't only humbling, it's motivating. When you live with the awareness that your choices ripple outward, strengthening others, you'll find the courage to keep walking in the light yourself.

## A Final Word of Hope

As this journey through pages and practices draws to a close, one truth must remain planted deep in your heart: You're loved with a love that won't let you go. Nothing (not relapse, not shame, not failure, not fear) can separate you from the love of God.[14] That love has carried you this far, and it won't abandon you now.

There may still be days of weakness, when old temptations linger and the shadows beckon. Don't despair. A stumble isn't the end of the road. Each morning dawns with mercy new and fresh.[15] Every sunrise is an invitation to begin again, to step once more into the grace that holds you steady. You're never back at square one, for every step you've taken with God is held in eternity, never wasted, never erased.

Lift your eyes, then, to the horizon of hope. You weren't created to live chained or diminished. You were crafted for freedom, peace, and joy.[16] The God who breathed life into you is still breathing, still guiding, still shaping you for good works and holy purpose. What you thought was ruin has become the soil of redemption.[17] What you thought was the end has become the beginning of a new story.

13. Matt 28:18–20.
14. Rom 8:38–39.
15. Lam 3:22–23.
16. John 10:10; Gal 5:1.
17. Gen 50:20.

So walk forward with confidence. Let your life testify to grace. Let your steps echo with courage. May the peace of God guard your heart. May the joy of Christ sustain your spirit. May the Spirit's power carry you further than you ever dreamed possible. And may you remember, always, that the One "who began this good work in you is faithful and will bring it to completion."[18]

This is your hope, your future, your promise: freedom unfolding, love unending, life abundant. Pause here, and let hope settle into your spirit: the journey continues, and the One who walks beside you will never let you go.[19]

## Reflection Questions

1. Looking back on my journey, where do I most clearly see God's grace sustaining me?
2. What lessons from my past struggles continue to shape the way I live today?
3. How do I sense God inviting me into deeper dependence and growth in this next season?
4. When setbacks come, what truths or Scriptures remind me that recovery is lifelong and grace never ends?

## Action Steps

1. Begin a short daily practice of gratitude, naming one way you've seen God's presence in your recovery.
2. Write down one lesson from your recovery journey that you want to carry forward into the next season.
3. Share your story of perseverance with one trusted person this week as a way of encouraging both them and yourself.
4. End each day with a simple prayer of dependence: "God, thank you for carrying me today. Lead me in your love tomorrow."

18. Phil 1:6.
19. Heb 13:5; Deut 31:8.

# Epilogue

## A Prayer and Benediction

Beloved, go now in the freedom Christ has won.
You're no longer defined by chains, but by grace.
No longer named by shame, but by love.
No longer bound by the past, but alive to a future full of hope.

May mercy meet you in your weakness.
May strength rise in your surrender.
May joy surprise you in the ordinary.
And may peace guard your heart in every storm.

Go as a child of God:
redeemed, renewed, unshackled.
And may the blessing of the Father, the Son, and the Holy Spirit
rest upon you and remain with you,
now and always.

Amen.

# Rationale for the Order of the Appendices

I've included the six appendices to deepen the reader's experience, offering both theological grounding and practical tools for personal and communal recovery. They extend the core message of the book (freedom through Christ) into tangible resources, reflections, and actions that support lasting transformation beyond the final chapter.

The ordering of the appendices follows a thoughtful and pastoral progression, designed to support the reader's journey through spiritual recovery and ongoing transformation. It begins with **framework**: Appendix A offers a clear and honest exploration of how the Twelve Steps align with and differ from a Christ-centered theological vision, bridging familiarity and faith. It then turns to **legitimacy**: Appendix B draws on the best of contemporary addiction science to affirm the book's spiritual approach through interdisciplinary insights. From there, the lens widens to **context**: Appendix C addresses the systemic, structural, and cultural forces in Western societies that fuel and sustain addiction, calling for both personal healing and social change. The focus then becomes deeply **personal and reflective**: Appendix D provides inventories and assessments to help readers name their struggles and track growth with clarity and grace. Next, the trajectory moves outward toward **community and equipping**: Appendix E offers resources for sponsors, mentors, and support groups who walk alongside those in recovery, equipping them with pastoral wisdom and practical tools. Finally, the journey culminates in **prayerful grounding**: Appendix F invites the reader to linger with Scripture meditations and recovery-focused prayers that nourish the soul and sustain transformation.

These appendices have been added to extend the reach of the main chapters, providing practical, theological, personal, and communal resources that help readers not only understand but also embody the recovery journey. Together, they reflect the book's commitment to holistic, grace-filled, and Christ-centered healing.

# Appendix A

# Walking with the Twelve Steps

*Unshackled: Breaking Addiction's Chains* through God's Grace shares many parallels with the well-known Twelve Steps of Alcoholics Anonymous (AA). These steps have helped millions find sobriety, connection, and purpose through an intentional spiritual journey. While *Unshackled* is explicitly Christ-centered and deeply rooted in Christian theology, it aligns with many of the principles and practices at the heart of AA and its offshoots. This appendix outlines key points of alignment and divergence, and offers resources for further study for those interested in integrating both approaches.

## Areas of Strong Alignment

| AA Step | Theme | *Unshackled* Alignment |
|---|---|---|
| Step 1 | Powerlessness | Ch. 1: Recognizing the grip of addiction and human frailty |
| Step 2 | Belief in Higher Power | Ch. 2: Faith in God's power to restore |
| Step 3 | Surrender | Ch. 2: Turning one's life and will over to God |
| Step 4 | Moral Inventory | Chs. 4 and 6: Honest self-examination and relational assessment |
| Step 5 | Confession | Chs. 4 and 6: Confession to God and others for healing |
| Steps 6 and 7 | Removal of Defects | Ch. 4: Prayers for transformation and sanctification |

| AA Step | Theme | *Unshackled* Alignment |
|---|---|---|
| Steps 8 and 9 | Amends | Ch. 6: Ownership, restitution, and reconciliation |
| Step 10 | Daily Inventory | Ch. 7: Ongoing surrender, reflection, and honesty |
| Step 11 | Prayer and Meditation | Ch. 7 and Appendix: Daily prayer and Scripture reflection |
| Step 12 | Service and Mission | Ch. 8: Witness, purpose, and community service |

**Table 1: Areas of Strong Alignment with the Twelve Steps of Alcoholics Anonymous**

## Core Differences

- **Theological specificity**: While AA encourages belief in a "higher power," *Unshackled* names Jesus Christ as Lord and Savior. The Christian gospel is the foundation for all healing and transformation described in this book.
- **Scriptural authority**: *Unshackled* relies on Scripture as the primary guide for life, recovery, and discipleship, whereas AA draws more broadly from spiritual traditions.
- **View of sin and redemption**: *Unshackled* frames addiction as a spiritual bondage resulting from sin and human brokenness, calling for redemption through grace. AA tends to describe addiction as a disease or moral injury without the same theological framing.

## Where AA Complements *Unshackled*

Readers who resonate with *Unshackled* may find great value in twelve-step meetings for community support, structure, and accountability. Programs like Celebrate Recovery (Christ-centered) and Alcoholics Anonymous (spiritually open) can reinforce the practices laid out in this book.

# Appendix B

# Addiction Recovery and Modern Research

Modern addiction science affirms much of what *Unshackled* teaches from a theological and spiritual perspective. Today, researchers and clinicians increasingly adopt a biopsychosocial-spiritual model, acknowledging that recovery requires transformation of body, mind, relationships, and spirit. This appendix summarizes key research-aligned principles in *Unshackled*, along with areas of theological distinction and recommended resources for further learning.

## Major Areas of Agreement

| Research Area | Scientific Insight | *Unshackled* Parallel |
|---|---|---|
| Trauma and Addiction | Addiction often masks unresolved trauma (Maté, Van der Kolk) | Chs. 1 and 4: Emotional wounding and healing in Christ |
| Neuroplasticity and Thought Patterns | The brain can be rewired through repetition, belief, and habit change | Ch. 3: Renewing the mind with God's truth |
| Social Connection | Connection reduces relapse; isolation fuels addiction | Chs. 6 and 8: Fellowship, accountability, and church community |
| Spiritual Coping | Faith reduces relapse, increases resilience | Entire book: Recovery through surrender, prayer, and spiritual formation |

| Research Area | Scientific Insight | *Unshackled* Parallel |
|---|---|---|
| Habit Formation | Long-term change requires daily disciplines and structure | Ch. 7: New habits, rhythms, and lifestyle patterns |
| Self-Compassion and Forgiveness | Crucial to reduce shame and support healing | Chs. 5 and 6: Grace, forgiveness of self and others |

**Table 2: Areas of Agreement With Modern Addiction Science**

## Therapeutic Modalities and Clinical Approaches

Modern recovery research supports the use of various evidence-based therapies:

- **Cognitive Behavioral Therapy** (**CBT**) helps individuals identify and reframe negative thought patterns and behaviors.
- **Dialectical Behavior Therapy** (**DBT**) supports emotional regulation, distress tolerance, and relational skills.
- **Eye Movement Desensitization and Reprocessing** (**EMDR**) is effective in treating trauma, which often underlies addiction.
- **Motivational Interviewing** (**MI**) helps build internal motivation for change without judgment.
- **Trauma-Informed Therapy** emphasizes safety, empowerment, and understanding of past harm.

*Unshackled* aligns with these modalities through its emphasis on renewing thought patterns, healing emotional wounds, fostering relational skills, and offering hope. While it doesn't name these therapies directly, many of its spiritual practices reflect similar principles and goals.

## Pharmacological and Medical Treatments

Medical approaches to addiction are an important aspect of recovery for many:

- **Medication-Assisted Treatment** (**MAT**) using drugs like buprenorphine, methadone, or naltrexone can help manage cravings and withdrawal.

- **Psychiatric care** can address co-occurring mental health disorders such as depression, anxiety, or PTSD.
- **Detox and inpatient care** provide safe environments for early recovery.

*Unshackled* doesn't address these directly, but its spiritual and theological model can be a powerful complement to medical and therapeutic care. Readers are encouraged to seek integrated care with professionals who respect their faith and healing journey.

## Areas of Theological Distinction

- **Sin and redemption**: Scientific literature often avoids moral or theological language, while *Unshackled* embraces it as central to healing.
- **Deliverance and spiritual warfare**: Secular research doesn't engage the demonic or spiritual strongholds, but these are included as real dynamics in *Unshackled.*
- **Divine agency**: Recovery is framed not just as a human effort but as God's active work of grace and transformation.

## How to Integrate Both

- Many readers will benefit from both clinical recovery programs and spiritual practices. Therapy, medication-assisted treatment (MAT), support groups, and trauma-informed care can be **complemented** by the Christ-centered approach of *Unshackled.*
- I encourage readers to consult Christian therapists or trauma specialists who understand both neuroscience and theology.

Appendices A and B are offered to strengthen the integration of faith and research, spiritual wisdom and clinical insight. They underscore the profound harmony between Scripture, lived experience, and the growing body of evidence in addiction science and recovery support.

# Appendix C

## Addressing Societal and Structural Factors Perpetuating Addictions

Addiction is often portrayed as a personal failing or a family problem, but evidence shows that it's deeply embedded in broader social contexts. In Western nations, a range of institutional, structural, systemic, cultural, and governmental factors can cause, perpetuate, accentuate, or sustain addictions, whether to substances (like alcohol and drugs) or behaviors (such as gambling, work, sex, or pornography).[1]

Focusing solely on individual willpower or family circumstances overlooks these wider forces. Indeed, widespread addiction is a relatively modern phenomenon, not explained by sudden changes in human biology, but by changes in society itself.[2] Traditional social institutions (families, schools, communities, even religious and civic organizations) that once helped protect against addiction have weakened in their influence.[3]

This appendix presents an analysis of how larger issues in Western culture and society contribute to addiction, and recommends changes necessary to address them comprehensively. Although this appendix primarily focuses on the structural and cultural dynamics within Western societies, its analysis and recommendations have broader relevance. Many of the systemic drivers of addiction (such as economic inequality, social fragmentation, and exploitative industry practices) manifest in diverse ways across

1. El Hayek et al., "Stigma Toward Substance Use Disorders."

2. Westermeyer, "Role of Cultural and Social Factors"; Lin et al., "Scoping Review of Social Determinants."

3. Westermeyer, "Role of Cultural and Social Factors."

the globe. Readers in Majority World contexts are invited to adapt and apply these insights to their settings, discerning how local cultural, political, and economic forces may similarly impact addiction and recovery.

## Institutional Factors (Healthcare, Education, and Workplace)

At the institutional level, Western societies face critical shortcomings in how major institutions address addiction. The healthcare system is a prime example. Addiction treatment historically has been segregated from mainstream healthcare, resulting in care that's often unequal, stigmatized, and inaccessible.[4] Many countries lack sufficient clinics, trained professionals, or insurance coverage for addiction services, making help hard to get. Although laws in the United States and elsewhere mandate parity (equal coverage) for substance use treatment, these laws are frequently unenforced.[5] As a result, people with addictions often fall through the cracks, receiving inadequate medical support. Moreover, many healthcare providers have harbored stigma toward patients with addiction, sometimes viewing them as difficult or morally failing.[6] Until recently, a "punish, don't treat" attitude prevailed, in part due to the legacy of the drug war.[7] This institutional stigma discourages clinicians from specializing in addiction medicine and deters patients from seeking help. To its credit, the medical community is slowly shifting to view addiction as a medical disorder rather than a personal moral failing, for example, replacing judgmental labels ("clean" or "dirty") with clinical terms like "in recovery" or "relapse."[8] However, much work remains to integrate addiction care fully into health systems.

Educational institutions also play a role. Schools and universities in Western nations have a mixed record on preventing addiction. Traditional curricula may include drug education, but often these programs are limited or didactic. In many communities, young people still lack practical life skills or mental health literacy that could help them cope with stress and avoid self-medicating with substances. At the same time, campus cultures sometimes unintentionally encourage addictive behaviors, for instance, binge drinking is widely acknowledged as a problem on many Western college

4. Koh, "What Led to the Opioid Crisis"; Rehman et al., "Structural Stigma Within Inpatient Care."

5. Koh, "What Led to the Opioid Crisis."

6. Leon Tesani, "How Stigma Affects Patients Seeking Help."

7. Grinspoon, "Poverty, Homelessness, and Social Stigma."

8. Koh, "What Led to the Opioid Crisis"; Rundle et al., "Examining the Relationship."

campuses, reflecting a gap between formal education about alcohol and the social environment students encounter. A strong institutional response would involve not only better health education but also creating campus policies and cultures that reduce heavy drinking and drug use (for example, restricting alcohol marketing on campus and providing appealing alcohol-free social events). At the primary and secondary school level, early intervention is critical: Identifying at-risk youth (such as those with trauma or learning difficulties) and providing counseling can mitigate later substance abuse. If schools lack resources such as guidance counselors or psychologists (a common situation due to budget constraints) then this protective institutional function is weakened. In summary, education systems in the West must be strengthened to offer both prevention and early support in the face of addiction risks.

The workplace is another institution where addiction intersects with structural issues. Western work culture often prizes long hours and productivity, which can sometimes blur into work addiction or enable substance misuse as a stress-coping mechanism. Many employers, however, have historically responded to addiction punitively (e.g., firing employees who fail drug tests) rather than supportively. This doesn't only harm individuals but also ignores root causes. Surveys indicate a large portion of US employers have experienced workplace incidents related to employee opioid use (accidents, absenteeism, etc.).[9] Yet, relatively few offer comprehensive Employee Assistance Programs or benefits for addiction treatment.[10] Progressive employers are beginning to recognize that they have a critical role in addressing addiction by offering health coverage for treatment, peer support groups at work, and non-punitive policies.[11] When workplaces fail to support employees' recovery, those struggling with addiction may lose their jobs and income, further exacerbating their problems.[12] Institutional support from employers and labor organizations (such as reasonable accommodations for treatment or recovery programs) is thus an essential piece of the puzzle.

Finally, other community institutions (like religious organizations, neighborhood groups, and civic associations) historically provided social support and a sense of belonging that shielded individuals from addictive behaviors.[13] In contemporary Western societies, many of these traditional

9. Akanbi et al., "Systematic Review."
10. Kim et al., "Opioid Crisis"; Merrefield, "Mental Health Care at Work."
11. Kim et al., "Opioid Crisis."
12. Wine, "Addiction in the Workplace."
13. Westermeyer, "Role of Cultural and Social Factors."

community bonds have become weaker. Urbanization, secularization, and mobility mean that individuals may lack the tight-knit community safety nets that once provided for those in distress. The decline of these protective institutions doesn't imply that the answer lies in retreating to the past; instead, it suggests society must find new ways for institutions to fill the void, for example, community centers, support groups, and secular nonprofits can recreate some of the protective social fabric that helps prevent isolation and addiction.

## Structural and Systemic Factors (Socioeconomic and Policy Structures)

Broader structural forces in society significantly shape addiction patterns. Chief among these are the social determinants of health, which refer to the socioeconomic conditions in which people live and work. Poverty, inequality, unemployment, and lack of stable housing all heighten the risk of addiction and worsen its outcomes. Studies consistently find that drug-related deaths and problems concentrate in economically disadvantaged communities.[14] For example, one analysis of US data (2002–2014) showed opioid overdose rates were significantly higher in zip codes with more poverty and unemployment and lower median incomes and education levels.[15] Homelessness, too, is strongly associated with overdose risk.[16] These patterns aren't coincidences; they reveal how structural economic dislocation and social stress can drive people toward substance use as a coping mechanism and create environments where addiction spirals. When good jobs are unavailable and social mobility is stalled, some individuals (especially those facing physical or emotional pain) may turn to readily available sources of escape (whether drugs, alcohol, or behavioral vices) in the absence of hope or opportunity. In this way, economic inequality and lack of social support act as fuel for addiction. Any serious societal response to addiction must therefore grapple with underlying issues like poverty, joblessness, and affordable housing. As Dr. Peter Grinspoon observed, losing housing or income can destabilize even a person in long-term recovery, making relapse far more likely.[17] Strengthening the social safety net (through measures like housing assistance, employment programs, and equitable economic policies) is a structural strategy to reduce the grip of addiction.

14. Lin et al., "Scoping Review of Social Determinants."
15. Grinspoon, "Poverty, Homelessness, and Social Stigma."
16. Grinspoon, "Poverty, Homelessness, and Social Stigma."
17. Grinspoon, "Poverty, Homelessness, and Social Stigma."

Another pervasive structural factor is systemic discrimination, particularly systemic racism. In Western countries such as the United States, Australia, and Canada, minority communities have often borne the brunt of punitive drug policies and inadequate access to care. The "War on Drugs," launched in the twentieth century, disproportionately targeted Black, Indigenous, and other people of color, framing addiction in those communities as a criminal issue rather than a health issue.[18] The result has been generations of marginalized individuals facing incarceration instead of treatment, fractured trust in authorities, and intergenerational trauma. Even today, structural and institutional racism persist in how addiction services are delivered.[19] A 2022 Canadian study on harm reduction services found that "structural and institutional racism are prevalent," with ostensibly "colorblind" policies failing to reach Black and Indigenous people in need.[20] The very design of services often centers on the majority population, leaving minorities feeling unwelcome or distrustful. This points to a broader truth: Structural racism and bias in institutions create barriers to access, whether it's fewer clinics in minority neighborhoods, culturally insensitive treatment programs, or law enforcement practices that punish some groups more harshly for the same behaviors.[21] Overcoming addiction at a societal level will require intentional efforts to advance equity, such as culturally tailored interventions, diversifying the addiction workforce, and policy reforms that undo racist legacies (for instance, revising drug sentencing laws that disproportionately imprison people of color).

Significantly, many systemic issues are reinforced by policy choices and powerful interests. In some cases, corporate profit motives and government policies have combined to exacerbate addiction epidemics. The opioid crisis is a stark illustration: Pharmaceutical companies like Purdue Pharma aggressively marketed opioid painkillers (such as OxyContin) while downplaying addiction risks, and regulators (the FDA) approved these drugs and allowed their proliferation with insufficient safeguards.[22] A post-mortem analysis characterized the opioid epidemic as a "multi-system failure of regulation" (from approval of misleading drug labels to weak oversight of physician education) all influenced by industry pressure and lobbying.[23]

18. Godkhindi et al., "They're Causing More Harm than Good."

19. El Hayek et al., "Stigma Toward Substance Use Disorders."

20. Godkhindi et al., "They're Causing More Harm Than Good."

21. Tyndall and Dodd, "How Structural Violence, Prohibition, and Stigma."

22. Koh, "What Led to the Opioid Crisis"; Rehman et al., "Structural Stigma within Inpatient Care."

23. Koh, "What Led to the Opioid Crisis."

Even after approval, much responsibility for physician training about opioids was left to the drug manufacturers themselves, a situation ripe for conflict of interest.[24] Donations from opioid makers to politicians and a "revolving door" between regulators and industry further skewed policies in favor of industry interests over public health.[25] These systemic regulatory gaps helped create an environment where millions became addicted to prescription opioids, leading to a wave of heroin and fentanyl use when the prescriptions were curtailed. Thus, addiction can be seen as a symptom of deeper system failures: in this case, failures of governance, ethics, and corporate accountability.

The gambling industry offers a parallel example. With the rise of legalized gambling (casinos, lotteries, and online betting) in Western countries, governments and companies have profited tremendously, but often at the expense of public health. In the United States, after sports betting was legalized in 2018, gambling firms rushed into new markets and have lobbied aggressively against consumer protection regulations intended to curb addiction.[26] A 2025 watchdog report revealed that major betting companies opposed proposals, including limits on advertising, caps on betting deposits, and bans on certain high-risk wager types.[27] Industry lobbyists even argued that restricting particularly addictive forms of betting (like rapid in-game bets) would unduly cut into state tax revenues, framing public health measures as a threat to government income.[28] In several cases, these lobbying efforts succeeded in blocking or diluting regulations, highlighting a structural tension: governments come to rely on revenue from potentially addictive industries (gambling, alcohol, etc.), which may discourage strict regulation.

In my country, Australia, the government has faced sustained criticism for its handling of gambling, particularly due to its regulatory leniency and financial entanglement in the industry. Critics argue that governments at both state and federal levels have prioritized revenue over public health, given their significant earnings from taxes on pokies, casinos, and sports betting. This reliance creates a troubling conflict of interest, where efforts to curb gambling-related harm are often diluted or delayed. Advocacy groups and researchers have also pointed to insufficient support for prevention and recovery programs, despite rising rates of gambling addiction and the disproportionate impact on vulnerable communities.

24. Koh, "What Led to the Opioid Crisis."
25. Koh, "What Led to the Opioid Crisis."
26. Betts, "US Gambling Firms."
27. Betts, "US Gambling Firms."
28. Betts, "US Gambling Firms."

The same dynamic is seen with the alcohol and tobacco sectors, where Western governments impose taxes and enjoy revenue, while often stopping short of stronger controls on marketing or distribution. The World Health Organization has pointed out a "glaring gap" in alcohol marketing regulation globally.[29] Despite alcohol's known harms, advertising controls are "much weaker" compared to other harmful products, allowing alcohol companies to target young people and heavy drinkers freely. Digital media and cross-border advertisements now inundate vulnerable populations with pro-alcohol messaging, and international coordination to rein in such marketing is lacking.[30] All of this reflects how policy and economic structures can create addictive environments: through lax regulation, collusion with industry, or contradictory goals within government (such as public health versus revenue).

Structural and systemic issues (from economic inequality and racism to corporate influence on policy) form the underlying context in which addictions flourish. These factors often interact. For instance, an economically depressed neighborhood might also be one where liquor stores and betting shops cluster (a phenomenon sometimes termed "environmental injustice"), and where residents face both unemployment and targeted advertising for alcohol or payday casinos. Breaking the cycle of addiction, therefore, demands structural changes: reducing inequalities, redesigning policies that currently prioritize punishment or profit over wellness, and rebuilding social systems that give individuals stable, healthy ground on which to stand.

## Cultural Factors (Norms, Stigma, and Social Attitudes)

Culture profoundly shapes how addiction begins and how society responds to it. Western cultures have mixed messages when it comes to addictive substances and behaviors. On one hand, there is a long-standing cultural stigma around addiction: an attitude that views people with addictions as morally weak or self-indulgent. This stigma manifests in pejorative language (calling someone a "junkie" or "alcoholic" in a derogatory way) and in social ostracism. It has been reinforced by decades of criminalization of drug use, which implies that people who use certain drugs are criminals deserving punishment. The effect of stigma is harmful—it creates shame that can deter individuals from admitting their problem or seeking treatment, and it reduces public empathy, making it politically easier to ignore or

29. World Health Organization, "WHO Highlights Glaring Gaps."

30. World Health Organization, "WHO Highlights Glaring Gaps."

criminalize addiction rather than fund treatment.[31] As one analysis noted, laws and cultural norms have "encoded" stigma into the system, placing blame on individuals and reducing support for compassionate policies.[32] For example, when society labels addiction as solely a personal failing, there is less appetite to invest taxpayer money in rehabilitation programs; after all, the stigmatizing logic goes, "if they brought it on themselves, why should we help?" Fortunately, cultural attitudes are slowly evolving. There is growing recognition in Western countries that addiction is a complex medical and social issue. Public figures speaking about their recovery and media campaigns about the opioid crisis have somewhat softened attitudes. Still, a significant amount of stigma persists.[33] Overcoming that stigma is both a cultural and institutional project—it involves changing everyday language and portrayal of addiction, as well as ensuring public policies don't reinforce shame (for instance, by treating addiction in the health system rather than the criminal system).

Ironically, even as some addictions are heavily stigmatized, Western culture also normalizes or even glamorizes other addictive behaviors. Alcohol is a prime example. Drinking is woven into the social fabric (from college parties to networking events to family celebrations), making abstinence socially challenging. Advertising and entertainment industries further entrench alcohol's cultural status. Alcohol ads portray it as fun, sophisticated, or manly, and sports events are sponsored by beer and liquor brands. This normalization can mask the potential for addiction and discourage people from seeing heavy drinking as a problem. These cultural cues especially influence youth, and evidence shows that aggressive alcohol marketing contributes to earlier and heavier drinking among young people.[34]

A similar pattern is emerging with gambling: once frowned upon, gambling is now marketed as an exciting pastime, especially with online betting apps that sponsor sports teams and inundate the public with commercials. The cultural narrative shifts to "gambling as entertainment," downplaying the real risk of addiction for a significant minority of users. In the realm of behavioral addictions like workaholism, Western culture's strong emphasis on productivity and career success can lead to praise for unhealthy work habits. Someone working seventy-hour weeks may be lauded as ambitious rather than gently guided to seek balance. This cultural valorization of

31. Rundle et al., "Examining the Relationship."

32. Tyndall and Dodd, "How Structural Violence, Prohibition, and Stigma."

33. Grinspoon, "Poverty, Homelessness, and Social Stigma."

34. World Health Organization, "WHO Highlights Glaring Gaps"; El Hayek et al., "Stigma Toward Substance Use Disorders."

overwork makes it challenging to recognize when a work habit crosses into a compulsive behavior that damages one's health or family life.

Digital technology has also changed Western cultural patterns in ways relevant to addiction. Pornography and sexual content, once relatively inaccessible, are now available on personal devices to anyone, including adolescents, with minimal restriction. The cultural taboo around discussing pornography means many individuals consume it in secrecy, which can facilitate compulsive use without accountability or open conversation. While porn addiction (often termed "compulsive sexual behavior") is still debated in clinical terms, it's clear that easy access has increased the prevalence of problematic use for some, and society has yet to fully grapple with how to address it. A consumerist, individualistic cultural lens often treats sex or porn as just another personal choice, leaving those who feel controlled by these behaviors unsure where to turn, especially if they fear moral judgment.

More broadly, Western cultures have witnessed a decline in communal and spiritual frameworks that once provided individuals with a sense of meaning and belonging beyond material or immediate pleasures. This isn't to advocate a return to any specific religion. Still, sociologists note that factors such as community engagement, family cohesion, and clear moral or existential meaning can protect against addiction by fulfilling human needs in healthier ways.[35] Modern culture, with its fast pace and emphasis on the self, can foster alienation or existential voids that some fill with substances or addictive activities. The concept of "pleasure-seeking" is often celebrated (think of marketing slogans like "treat yourself" or "YOLO: you only live once"), which, in moderation, is fine; however, it can tilt into self-medication or escapism in the absence of balanced coping strategies.

Western cultural attitudes present a paradox, stigmatizing people who become addicted yet normalizing many of the behaviors and consumer goods that can lead to addiction. Changing this requires cultural reflection and public dialogue. Reducing stigma involves humanizing addiction: sharing success stories of recovery, educating people that addiction isn't simply a lack of willpower. At the same time, promoting a healthier culture might involve re-evaluating how we market and celebrate potentially addictive products. For example, some public health experts have called for banning or severely limiting alcohol advertising, similar to the way cigarette ads were curtailed, because evidence links ads with higher consumption and addiction risk.[36] Likewise, normalizing work-life balance and self-care over workaholism, or encouraging open family discussions about online

35. Westermeyer, "Role of Cultural and Social Factors."

36. Giesbrecht et al., "Impacts of Alcohol Marketing."

pornography and its effects, are cultural shifts that could help. A culture that values well-being and connection over excessive consumption and competition would be one less conducive to addiction.

## Governmental and Policy Issues

Government policy and action (or inaction) are often the deciding factors in either perpetuating addictions or mitigating them. One of the clearest lessons from the past century is that a punitive, criminal-justice-focused approach to addiction has failed. The US-led "War on Drugs" stands as a cautionary tale of well-intentioned policy yielding disastrous results. Despite decades of strict laws and policing intended to discourage drug use, drug addiction, and overdose rates have surged rather than diminished. The enforcement-heavy approach filled prisons with nonviolent drug offenders (disproportionately from minority communities) and inflicted collateral damage such as violent black markets and drug-related stigma.[37] Even amid the opioid overdose crisis, which has been declared a public health emergency, many drug policy laws remained stuck in the punitive paradigm.[38] The criminalization of people who use drugs not only leads to incarceration but also marginalization, isolation, entrenched poverty, and a vicious cycle of trauma, as noted in an analysis of North America's overdose epidemic.[39] In effect, drug laws themselves have often become a form of structural violence: social arrangements that put specific populations in harm's way.[40] For example, by making a substance illegal, policymakers can justify denying people basic health interventions (like clean syringes or safe injection sites) because helping might appear to "condone" illegal behavior.[41] This has led to absurd situations where proven harm-reduction measures are blocked, even though we would never consider withholding lifesaving measures in any other health epidemic.[42] The outcome of such policies is tragically predictable: continued high rates of drug use and overdose, transmission of diseases like HIV in the absence of syringe exchange, and people cycling in and out of jail without access to treatment.[43] Western governments must come to terms with this reality. Some are starting to. For instance, Portugal

37. Tyndall and Dodd, "How Structural Violence, Prohibition, and Stigma."
38. Tyndall and Dodd, "How Structural Violence, Prohibition, and Stigma."
39. Tyndall and Dodd, "How Structural Violence, Prohibition, and Stigma."
40. Tyndall and Dodd, "How Structural Violence, Prohibition, and Stigma."
41. Tyndall and Dodd, "How Structural Violence, Prohibition, and Stigma."
42. Tyndall and Dodd, "How Structural Violence, Prohibition, and Stigma."
43. Tyndall and Dodd, "How Structural Violence, Prohibition, and Stigma."

famously decriminalized personal possession of all drugs in 2001 and invested in treatment, seeing drops in overdose deaths and HIV infections as a result. Similarly, several Western European countries have embraced harm reduction (providing supervised consumption sites, heroin-assisted treatment, etc.) as part of policy, with positive outcomes. These examples demonstrate that government policies grounded in public health rather than punishment can yield more effective results.

Aside from drug laws, government regulation of legal addictive substances and activities is another key issue. As discussed earlier, regulatory gaps exist in areas like alcohol marketing and gambling expansion. Governments have the authority to set the rules for industries through taxation, age restrictions, advertising limits, and other controls. When those controls are lax or influenced by industry lobbying, the public can pay the price. For example, in many Western countries, alcohol excise taxes haven't kept pace with inflation or with alcohol's real social cost, making alcoholic drinks relatively cheaper and more accessible, especially to heavy drinkers (who are price-sensitive). Stronger policies, like minimum unit pricing for alcohol (implemented in Scotland, for instance) or mandates for plain packaging and health warnings (as done for tobacco), are available tools that governments can use to curb excessive consumption. Yet political will is often lacking until a crisis point is reached.

The role of government funding and infrastructure for addiction treatment is also pivotal. Addictions can't be addressed solely by the private sector or charities; comprehensive public systems are needed. Western nations vary widely in this regard. Some countries (like France or Switzerland) have robust public treatment services and socialized healthcare that includes addiction care. Others, such as the United States, rely on a patchwork of private clinics, insurance-based care, and underfunded public programs. The result is that many people who want help can't get it. In the United States, it's estimated that only a fraction of those with a substance use disorder receive specialty treatment in a given year, often because of cost, lack of providers, or stigma. Government initiatives to expand treatment access (such as funding community clinics, supporting medication-assisted treatment for opioid use disorder, and training more addiction specialists) are essential. Notably, the expansion of Medicaid under the Affordable Care Act led to more people getting addiction treatment and was correlated with reduced overdose death rates in states that expanded Medicaid.[44] This underscores that policy decisions about healthcare funding save lives when it comes to addiction. Similarly, when governments fund housing-first programs or job

44. Koh, "What Led to the Opioid Crisis."

training for individuals in recovery, those individuals have a significantly better chance of staying sober. Unfortunately, funding is often piecemeal and vulnerable to shifts in political priorities. Long-term, sustained investment is needed, since addiction is a chronic issue that doesn't respond to short-term grants or pilot projects alone.[45]

Another governmental issue is the coordination (or lack thereof) among different branches and levels of government. Addictions straddle multiple domains (criminal justice, health, education, and welfare) which in many countries are handled by various agencies that may not always work in concert. A person with addiction might simultaneously be on the radar of police, courts, social services, and healthcare providers. Yet, if these systems don't share information or collaborate, that person can fall through the gaps. Governments need integrated strategies that break down silos. For example, diverting individuals with drug-related offenses into treatment programs requires police, prosecutors, courts, and health services to have joint protocols and resources. It also means lawmakers should revisit any contradictory laws, for instance, at the federal level in the United States, marijuana remains illegal even as many states legalize it, creating conflicts in enforcement and messaging.

Governments play a crucial role in shaping public attitudes through effective leadership and the dissemination of accurate information. Officials who speak in terms of compassion and science (acknowledging addiction as an illness and a societal challenge) can help shift the public discourse. In contrast, political rhetoric that resorts to scare tactics or moral panic (e.g., characterizing drug users as a menace) can deepen divisions and stigma. Governments can also sponsor public education campaigns about addiction, similar to past campaigns on tobacco or HIV, emphasizing prevention and understanding.

Governmental change is often the linchpin for broader societal change on addiction. By reforming laws that have unintended harmful consequences, by regulating industries that profit from addictive behaviors, by funding the services that people need, and by leading with informed discourse, governments in Western nations can either continue to perpetuate the status quo or take bold steps to reduce addiction in the long run.

## Recommendations and Reforms

Addressing addiction requires more than tweaking individual behavior: it demands systemic reforms across various sectors of society. Based on the

45. Koh, "What Led to the Opioid Crisis."

analysis above, here are key recommendations to tackle the institutional, structural, cultural, and governmental issues that fuel addiction:

- **Reform drug policy and criminal justice.** Western governments should shift from punitive approaches to health-centered approaches. This means decriminalizing personal use and possession of drugs (to eliminate the fear and stigma that drive users underground) and expanding diversion programs that send people to treatment instead of jail. Evidence-based harm reduction strategies (such as needle exchange programs, medication-assisted therapy (e.g., methadone, buprenorphine), and supervised consumption sites) should be implemented widely, as they have proven to save lives and connect people to care.[46] Law enforcement resources can be re-focused on high-level trafficking and on directing people to services, rather than on arresting individuals for addiction itself. These changes would require updating laws, retraining police and judges, and investing in treatment infrastructure to handle the influx of people seeking help rather than being incarcerated.
- **Integrate and fund addiction treatment in healthcare.** Healthcare institutions must treat addiction as a chronic health condition. Hospitals and clinics should be equipped to initiate treatment (for example, start opioid addiction patients on buprenorphine in emergency departments) and provide referrals to ongoing care. Governments and insurers need to ensure parity by covering addiction and mental health services on par with other medical conditions, and enforcing that coverage.[47] Stable, long-term funding is essential, not just one-year or two-year grants. One recommendation from public health experts is to fully integrate addiction services into primary care and mental health care, so that every physician or healthcare provider has basic training in addiction and can screen and assist patients.[48] This also includes expanding the workforce: training more addiction medicine specialists, psychiatrists, and counselors, as well as empowering nurse practitioners and social workers in this field. By making treatment readily accessible (and affordable) for anyone who needs it, many addictions can be caught earlier and prevented from worsening.
- **Address social determinants.** Reducing the structural drivers of addiction means fighting poverty, inequality, and isolation. Policymakers

46. Tyndall and Dodd, "How Structural Violence, Prohibition, and Stigma."
47. Koh, "What Led to the Opioid Crisis."
48. Koh, "What Led to the Opioid Crisis."

should recognize that improving social conditions is a form of prevention and intervention for addiction. Concretely, this could involve: increasing the minimum wage and strengthening labor protections to reduce economic insecurity; investing in affordable housing to combat homelessness (and thus providing those with substance use disorders a stable environment, which is shown to improve recovery chances dramatically);[49] and expanding access to education and job training in marginalized communities, to offer alternatives and hope. Additionally, special attention is needed for communities ravaged by addiction epidemics (for example, former industrial towns hit hard by opioids). These areas might benefit from targeted economic redevelopment and public health outreach. Governments might create multi-agency "recovery task forces" in such regions, coordinating efforts in employment, healthcare, and law enforcement. By improving the baseline quality of life and reducing stressors in society, we remove some of the fertile ground in which addictions take root.

- **Consider cultural change and public education:** Combating the cultural aspects of addiction involves both grassroots and official efforts to change narratives. Public health campaigns can be launched to educate people about how addiction works: emphasizing that it can affect anyone and isn't a moral failure, which can chip away at stigma. These campaigns may feature stories of recovery and messages of empathy, and they should be disseminated to schools, workplaces, and the media to promote awareness and understanding. Schools should update their curricula to include not only warnings about drugs but also positive skill-building: teaching coping strategies, emotional resilience, and critical thinking about media/peer pressure. Communities can organize events and support groups (e.g., Alcoholics Anonymous, SMART Recovery, and other peer networks) that not only help those struggling but also visibly demonstrate that recovery is possible and supported. Meanwhile, responsible media representation is essential: filmmakers, journalists, and content creators in Western nations should be mindful of how they portray substance use and those with addiction (moving away from caricatures and tragedy-only storylines to more nuanced representations). On a different front, workplace culture should be addressed: Companies and governments can promote work-life balance by enforcing reasonable work-hour limits, encouraging use of vacation time, and discouraging the "glorification" of overwork. This can help prevent work addiction

49. Grinspoon, "Poverty, Homelessness, and Social Stigma."

and related burnout. For behavioral addictions like pornography or gaming, open conversations and age-appropriate education (such as discussing healthy sexuality and internet use with teens) can mitigate the shame and secrecy that often worsen these addictions.

- **Regulate and responsibilize industry.** Governments must hold industries that trade in potentially addictive goods more accountable for prevention and treatment. For example, impose tighter regulations on advertising of alcohol, gambling, and even emerging concerns like sports betting and cannabis, where legal, especially ads that target youth or mislead consumers about "safe" use.[50] Western nations could collaborate to regulate online marketing that crosses borders (as the WHO suggests) so that companies can't simply shift their advertising to less-regulated markets.[51] Furthermore, policymakers can require these industries to fund addiction services, much as tobacco taxes fund anti-smoking campaigns and healthcare, levies on alcohol and gambling revenues can support addiction treatment programs and research. Some US lawmakers have proposed using sports betting taxes to fund a national problem gambling initiative:[52] an idea that could be expanded. In the pharmaceutical realm, stronger oversight of drug marketing and aggressive penalization of misconduct (as seen in belated actions against opioid manufacturers) are necessary to deter future crises. Governments should also close the "revolving door" by which industry insiders unduly influence public policy, for instance, by lengthening mandatory cooling-off periods for regulators before they can work for companies they used to oversee.[53] Corporate social responsibility shouldn't be just a buzzword; industries ought to implement safeguards (like casino self-exclusion programs, or alcohol server training to refuse sale to intoxicated patrons) as standard practice, and governments should make them mandatory rather than voluntary.
- **Foster collaboration and innovative approaches.** Addressing a multifaceted issue like addiction requires collaboration across various sectors. Governments should convene task forces or commissions that include healthcare experts, social workers, law enforcement officials, community leaders, and individuals with lived experience of addiction to assess and guide policy continually. International knowledge-sharing among

50. Betts, "US Gambling Firms"; World Health Organization, "WHO Highlights Glaring Gaps."

51. World Health Organization, "WHO Highlights Glaring Gaps."

52. National Council on Problem Gambling, "Gambling Addiction."

53. Koh, "What Led to the Opioid Crisis."

Western nations can help spread innovations—for instance, learning from countries that have successful needle exchange or prescription heroin programs. Investment in research is also key: funding studies on pain management alternatives (to reduce over-reliance on opioids), on the impact of social media on behavioral addictions, and on what prevention strategies work best in different cultural contexts. Flexibility and local adaptation are crucial; what works in one community may need to be adjusted in another. By using data and piloting new ideas (like harm-reduction vending machines or mobile treatment units), societies can find more effective methods to reach those in need. In short, Western nations should treat the fight against addiction as an ongoing public health project, with the same rigor and urgency as efforts against other chronic diseases or epidemics.

## Conclusion

Addiction isn't an isolated personal issue; it's woven into the fabric of society. Western nations, in particular, face the challenge of rethinking deeply entrenched systems (from how we design cities and economies to how we educate youth and legislate drugs) to reduce the prevalence and harm of addiction. The analysis above illustrates that institutional failures, structural inequities, cultural attitudes, and policy missteps have all played a part in perpetuating addictive behaviors.

The hopeful news is that these are human-created problems, and thus within our power to change. By strengthening protective institutions (such as families, schools, healthcare, and community organizations), addressing social determinants, countering stigma, and enacting enlightened public policies, societies can create an environment where far fewer people develop destructive addictions.

The recommendations provided offer a road map grounded in research and successful examples, focusing on treating addiction as a health issue, investing in support systems, mitigating risks, and fostering a culture of empathy and balance. Such changes are ambitious and require sustained commitment, but the cost of inaction is evident in the lost lives and potential that addiction claims year after year.

Tackling the societal drivers of addiction isn't just an adjunct to personal recovery efforts; it's the necessary counterpart. In the end, freeing individuals from addiction ("unshackling" them, to invoke the language of liberation) will also free communities and future generations from one of the most pervasive sources of suffering in modern life. The task is complex, but the imperative is clear: to truly address addiction, Western societies must also heal themselves (their structures, values, and policies) creating a healthier environment in which both individuals and communities can thrive free of addiction's grasp.

# APPENDIX D

# Self-Assessments and Inventories for the Recovery Journey

## Addiction Impact Inventory

### Purpose

THIS TOOL HELPS YOU assess the cost of addiction across key areas of life: spiritual, relational, emotional, and physical. Addiction often inflicts widespread damage; it can undermine health, destabilize emotions, strain or break relationships, and create a deep spiritual void.[1] By recognizing these impacts, you can seek healing in each area.

### Instructions

For each domain below, reflect on how your addictive behavior has affected that aspect of your life. Write down specific consequences or losses you've experienced. You might rate the impact on a scale (e.g., 0 = no impact, 10 = severe impact) and jot examples. Be honest—the goal is awareness, not shame.

- **Spiritual life:** How has addiction affected your relationship with God and your sense of purpose? (E.g., feeling distant from God, loss of hope or meaning, neglecting prayer or worship.) Write down ways

1. Kiwi Recovery, "Overcoming Substance Use, Abuse and Chemical Dependency"; Howard, "2 Corinthians 5:17 and Addiction Recovery."

your faith life has been "hijacked" by addiction and any spiritual emptiness ("hole in the soul") you feel.[2]

- **Relationships:** Consider family, friends, church, and work relationships. Has trust been broken, or have you isolated yourself? List any relationships harmed by deceit, conflict, or neglect due to your addiction. (E.g., conflicts with a spouse, lost friendships, strained family ties). Who has been hurt or become distant?
- **Emotional/mental health:** How have your moods and mental well-being suffered? Many people experience heightened anxiety, depression, or shame during addiction.[3] Do you feel anger, guilt, or numbness more often? Note any mental health issues (anger outbursts, sadness, hopelessness, anxiety attacks) that have accompanied your substance use.
- **Physical health:** List the toll on your body. This can include medical problems (e.g., poor sleep, weight change, illnesses or injuries, withdrawal symptoms) and general self-care neglect. Has your energy or appearance changed? Have you experienced any doctor visits or health scares related to your use? Recognize the physical consequences (however minor or major) that have resulted from your addiction.

After writing, take a moment to review the overall picture. Addiction may have touched every corner of your life, but **awareness is the first step** toward healing. The losses you identify here can become motivation for change and prayer points as you invite God to restore what's been broken.[4]

## Denial and Minimization Checklist

### Purpose

Denial is a common defense mechanism in addiction: it "protects" us from painful reality by hiding or downplaying the truth. This checklist will help you spot subtle justifications and minimizations ("the lies we tell ourselves") that keep you stuck. By identifying these, you can counter each one with Scripture and truth, allowing light to replace the darkness of denial (John 8:32).

2. Samba Recovery, "Impact of Addiction on Spiritual Well-Being."
3. Kiwi Recovery, "Overcoming Substance Use, Abuse and Chemical Dependency."
4. Kiwi Recovery, "Overcoming Substance Use, Abuse and Chemical Dependency."

## Instructions

Read the list of common self-justifications below. Check any statement you've caught yourself thinking or saying. These are signs of denial or rationalization.[5] For each checked item, read the corresponding biblical truth provided and reflect on it (even write it out) to "take captive" that lie (2 Cor 10:5) and replace it with God's perspective.

## Common Justifications (Denial Statements)

- ☐ **"I can stop anytime I want."** *This classic denial assumes control, ignoring addiction's grip.* Truth: The Bible warns that we become "enslaved to whatever has mastered us."[6] Acknowledge that willpower alone isn't enough: you need God's help and possibly others' support to break free.
- ☐ **"I'm not hurting anyone but myself."** *This minimizes real damage to others.* Truth: Addiction harms loved ones emotionally, financially, and spiritually, even if indirectly. "None of us lives for ourselves alone" (Rom 14:7); your choices impact your family and community. (Consider how your relationships have suffered: denial keeps this hidden.)
- ☐ **"I need this to cope and I deserve some relief."** *This justifies the behavior as self-care.* Truth: Scripture invites us to cast our burdens on God (1 Pet 5:7) instead of false refuges. "The Lord is a refuge for the oppressed, a stronghold in times of trouble" (Ps 9:9). Real peace is found in God's presence, not a substance.
- ☐ **"I'll quit . . . just not right now."** *This is procrastination (the "tomorrow syndrome").*[7] Truth: "*Don't boast about tomorrow*" (Prov 27:1). The longer you put off change, the more entrenched the habit and consequences grow. God's word urges responding *today* when you hear God's voice (Heb 3:15).
- ☐ **"At least I'm better than ________."** (Comparing your use to others): *This deflects by finding someone "worse."* Truth: We're called to honest self-examination, not comparison. "Each one should test their actions . . . without comparing" (Gal 6:4). Your standard is God's best for you, not others' behavior.

5. Changes Addiction Rehab, "12 Patterns of Denial and Rationalising in Addiction."
6. Kelsey, "Celebrate Recovery Lesson One."
7. Changes Addiction Rehab, "12 Patterns of Denial and Rationalising in Addiction."

*. . . and any other arguments you tell yourself.* Write those down, too, and challenge them with truth. For example, **"I've tried before and can't change."** This is a despairing lie. Truth: "With God all things are possible" (Matt 19:26). As Scripture says, "You can't heal a wound by saying it's not there!"[8] Admitting the truth is hard, but it opens the door for Christ's healing. **Pray through each truth**, asking God to replace denial with clarity and honesty. Remember, God's truth sets us free (John 8:32). Freedom begins with facing reality in God's light.

## Spiritual Hunger Inventory

### Purpose

Addictive behaviors often emerge as misguided attempts to satisfy deep inner needs. This tool helps you examine your *spiritual longings*: the heart hungers (for love, peace, purpose, etc.) that may be fueling your addiction. Current research and Christian wisdom both note that beneath addiction's cravings is often a "chronic emptiness," a God-shaped void that substances or behaviors never fill.[9] Identifying these unmet spiritual needs will guide you to seek their true fulfillment in God rather than false substitutes.

### Instructions

In a quiet, prayerful mindset, use the prompts below to explore the spiritual desires and wounds of your heart. Be gently honest with yourself; this isn't about blame, but about understanding what your soul truly longs for. Write down your thoughts for each question. You may also journal a prayer in response, inviting God to meet you in each of your deepest needs.

- **Heart longings:** What do you find your soul "hungry" or thirsty for? List the core desires of your heart. Examples include love and acceptance, a sense of belonging, peace or relief from inner turmoil, purpose and meaning, joy or excitement, and comfort amid pain. (Think of Augustine's famous truth: "Our heart is restless until it rests in you"; we're designed such that our deepest happiness is found in God alone).[10] Which of these desires stands out to you right now? (Write as many as apply.)

8. Kelsey, "Celebrate Recovery Lesson One."
9. K., "Roots of Addiction"; Riccardi, "Augustine and Christian Longing."
10. Riccardi, "Augustine and Christian Longing."

___________________________________________

- **Misguided fillers:** In what ways have you been trying to satisfy those longings through your addiction or other unhealthy habits? For each longing above, jot down how substance use (or pornography, overeating, etc., if applicable) promised to meet that need. For example, "I drink or use drugs to feel accepted and confident socially" or "I looked at porn to escape feeling lonely." Be specific. This step may reveal why letting go is hard, because the addiction became a "poor substitute for love," a coping mechanism for unmet needs.[11]
- **The deeper cry:** What pain or emptiness might be driving these longings? Are there any wounds or past traumas that are linked to your spiritual hunger? (E.g., rejection in childhood leading to a craving for love; anxiety or grief leading to a craving for peace.) Note any significant life experiences that have left you feeling empty or fearful. Addiction expert Dr. Gabor Maté describes people with addiction as living in the "realm of hungry ghosts," driven by enormous appetites for security and love due to past deprivation.[12] What "hungry ghost" inside you needs compassion and healing?
- **True nourishment:** Reflect on how a relationship with God can address each of these needs. For each longing you listed, write a hopeful statement of how God's presence and promises could fill it. For example, "My heart longs for unconditional love: God says God loves me so much God sent Jesus to save me (John 3:16)." Or, "I seek purpose: God created me for good works and a hope (Eph 2:10, Jer 29:11)." Use Scripture if you can (perhaps draw from verses or stories that comfort you). If you're a new believer, you might look up promises in the Bible about God's love, peace, comfort, or purpose and note them here.

After this inventory, you should have a clearer picture of the spiritual "hole" you've been trying to fill. Many describe addiction as having a "God-sized hole" in the soul that only a relationship with God can truly fill.[13] Take time to pray over these findings. **Affirmation:** "Lord, you know my deepest longings. Teach me to bring my hungry heart to you. You promise, 'Blessed are those who hunger and thirst for righteousness, for they shall be filled' (Matt 5:6). Fill me with your love and spirit, as I seek you instead of __________." (Feel free to write your prayer.) Remember, "People can't live

11. K., "Roots of Addiction."

12. K., "Roots of Addiction."

13. K., "Roots of Addiction"; Samba Recovery, "Impact of Addiction on Spiritual Well-Being."

by bread alone, but by every word from the mouth of God" (Matt 4:4). Our souls live on God's presence and truth. This is the bread that truly satisfies.

## Readiness for Change Scale

### Purpose

This assessment gauges your current stage of readiness to change and helps you articulate your hopes and fears about recovery. Change is a journey, and psychological research (the Transtheoretical Model) describes stages people go through: **Pre-Contemplation**, **Contemplation**, **Preparation**, **Action**, **Maintenance**, and sometimes **Relapse.**[14] Identifying your stage can bring clarity. Additionally, reflecting on what excites you about recovery (your hopes) and what worries you (your fears) will prepare you to move forward with honesty and courage.[15] This tool blends proven behavioral science with personal journaling to help you commit to growth.

### Instructions

Read the stage descriptions below and mark which stage best describes you today. It's normal to move back and forth between stages; this isn't a test, just a snapshot of where your mind and heart are right now. Once you've identified your stage, use the journal prompts to explore your motivations, hopes, and fears. This can help you (and those supporting you) tailor your next steps in recovery. Be truthful; there's no "wrong" stage to be in. God can meet you wherever you are.

## Stages of Change (Which *One* Sounds Like You?)

- **Pre-Contemplation ("Not Ready"):** You aren't **yet considering** change. This is the denial stage. You might feel your addiction isn't a serious problem, or you're unwilling to give it up. Perhaps others are concerned, but you defend your habit and have no plan to quit soon.[16] (In AA terms, you're "in denial").

14. Arista Recovery, "Stages of Change in Addiction Recovery."
15. Arms Acres, "5 Common Fears in Recovery."
16. Arista Recovery, "Stages of Change in Addiction Recovery."

- **Contemplation ("Maybe I Should"):** You **acknowledge the problem** but feel ambivalent. You *think about* change, yet haven't committed. You're aware of pros and cons. You know something must eventually give, but you feel fear and uncertainty about quitting.[17] (You might say, "I *want* to stop feeling this way, but I'm not sure I'm ready to act").
- **Preparation ("Getting Ready"):** You are **deciding to change** and starting to plan. Perhaps you've set a quit date or started researching help options (such as detox, meetings, or counseling). You feel more resolved, even if still anxious. This stage often involves taking small steps (e.g., cutting down on use, confiding in someone, or eliminating a major trigger), as you build courage and develop practical strategies for managing your addiction.
- **Action ("Taking the Plunge"):** You are **actively working on recovery**. You've made clear changes. For example, you've stopped using substances (or are in treatment), you're attending recovery meetings or counseling, and you're avoiding old triggers. This stage requires the most energy and focus. You might be experiencing withdrawal or intense cravings, but you're fighting through with new behaviors and support.
- **Maintenance ("Staying on Track"):** You've maintained sobriety or new habits for a significant period (months or more) and are now focused on **preventing relapse** and growing in your new life. You still must be vigilant (complacency can be dangerous), but you have more confidence. You may be repairing relationships, developing healthy routines, and perhaps helping others. The key question here is how to sustain these changes in the long term.

*(Relapse is sometimes considered a separate "stage," acknowledging that slips can happen. If you have relapsed in the past, don't be discouraged; use that experience to strengthen your plan. This time, you can anticipate triggers and be better prepared).*[18]

## Journal Prompts

Now, based on your stage above, write down your thoughts on the following:

- **Hopes:** What are you looking forward to if you pursue recovery fully? List your hopes and positive motivations. (Examples: "I hope to

17. Arista Recovery, "Stages of Change in Addiction Recovery."
18. Arms Acres, "5 Common Fears in Recovery."

restore my health," "I want to rebuild trust with my family," "I'm looking forward to feeling God's presence again," "I want my self-respect back," or simply "freedom from this burden.") Dream a little: What freedom or blessings do you sense God wants to give you as you walk into sobriety? **"Recovery can bring ________."** Write whatever comes to mind. No hope is too small or too grand. This is your vision of the **"promised land"** ahead.

- **Fears:** It's natural to have fears about changing.[19] What fears or obstacles make you hesitate? Write them out bluntly. (Examples: "I'm afraid of withdrawal symptoms," "I fear I'll fail and relapse," "What if I lose friends?" "I don't know who I'm without this habit," or "Life might be boring sober"). Bring these into the open. God tells us, "Cast all your anxiety on God, because God cares for you" (1 Pet 5:7). As you list each fear, you might also write a quick prayer surrendering it. "I fear ________, but God, I give that fear to you: help me overcome it." Acknowledging fear is essential; as one recovery center notes, fear can motivate change, but it can also be a barrier if left unaddressed.[20] Shine light on those fears now.
- **Readiness commitment:** Given where you're at, what's one step you feel **ready** to take next? It could be tiny or big. Write a specific action tailored to your current stage. If you're in *Pre-Contemplation*: Maybe "I'll reread my impact inventory and pray for willingness to change." If in *Contemplation*: "I'll talk honestly with a pastor or counselor about my addiction for the first time." If in *Preparation*: "I'll set a quit date and ask a friend to hold me accountable," or "I'll arrange childcare while I attend rehab." If in *Action*: "I'll stick with my program and call my sponsor daily." If in *Maintenance*: "I'll join a ministry or recovery group to support others, and continue strengthening my sobriety." Seal it with a statement of commitment: "I'm willing to change, and my next step is ________." This is your personal "I'll" statement. Write it, say it aloud, and trust God for the courage to do it. "For God is working in you, giving you the desire and the power to do what pleases God" (Phil 2:13).

19. Arms Acres, "5 Common Fears in Recovery."
20. Arms Acres, "5 Common Fears in Recovery."

## God-Image and Self-Image Inventory

### Purpose

Addiction often distorts how we see God and ourselves. Shame and guilt can poison our self-image (we feel unlovable, worthless) and skew our God-image (we may view God as angry, punishing, or distant). Studies show that a **negative image of God** (seeing God as harsh or uncaring), can perpetuate addiction, whereas a **positive, loving image of God** is linked to better recovery outcomes.[21] Likewise, embracing our identity as beloved children of God is crucial for lasting change. This tool helps you surface those hidden beliefs and then realign them with Scripture. The goal is to replace lies with truth: to see God as God truly is (loving, just, gracious) and to see yourself as God sees you (precious enough that Christ died for you).

### Instructions

Below is a list of common statements reflecting distorted beliefs about God and self. Check any that resonate (even slightly) as feelings or thoughts you've had. Then, in the "Truth Reflection" section, you'll be guided to counter each checked belief with biblical truth. Take your time and be prayerful; let God's word renew your mind (Rom 12:2). You might find it powerful to write out a verse or affirmation that speaks to each lie you've believed.

### Beliefs About God (Check Any You've Felt)

- ☐ "God is disappointed in me most of the time."
- ☐ "I think God is punishing me or withholding blessings because of my addiction."
- ☐ "God has probably given up on me by now."
- ☐ "I can't approach God until I get my act together. I feel too unclean to come to God."
- ☐ "God might love other people, but God doesn't love me in a personal way."
- ☐ "I've sinned so much that God is angry with me. God must be tired of forgiving me."

21. Timmons, "Christian Faith-Based Recovery Theory."

Add your own, if any, in a similar format. Perhaps in honest moments, you've thought, "Does God care about my recovery?" or "God's tired of hearing me repent." Write those down too.

## Beliefs About Self (Check Any That Apply)

- ☐ "I'm a bad person/a failure."
- ☐ "I don't deserve to be loved. If people (or God) knew the real me, they'd reject me."
- ☐ "I'll always be an addict or screw-up; it's just who I'm."
- ☐ "I'm beyond forgiveness or hope."
- ☐ "I must earn God's love by being good. Until I conquer this, I'm not worthy of God."
- ☐ "There's something fundamentally wrong with me."

(Again, add any others that voice how you see yourself. Many in recovery struggle with core shame: "I'm not enough," "I'm broken," etc. Bring those thoughts into the open).

## Truth Reflection: Replacing Lies with God's Truth

Now, take each belief you checked and actively counter it. Below are **truth statements** found in Scripture. Read them slowly. For any lie you identified, find one or more truths here (or from your study) that address it. Write the truth out **in your handwriting** and say it aloud. Let these truths migrate from your head to your heart over time.

- **God's character:** "The **Lord** is compassionate and gracious, slow to anger, abounding in love" (Ps 103:8). God isn't eager to punish you; God is keen to forgive and embrace you. God's patience is far greater than your stubbornness. **Truth:** God's fundamental stance toward you is mercy and love, not perpetual anger.
- **God's promise:** "Never will I leave you; never will I forsake you" (Heb 13:5b). If you believed "God has given up on me," confront that with God's promise that God **won't abandon you**. In Christ, you are adopted (Eph 1:5): a son or daughter. A good father doesn't disown his

child for struggling; he helps. **Truth:** God is with you in this struggle, not against you.[22]

- **Your worth:** You are **made in God's image**: this gives you inherent worth (Gen 1:27). Yes, our likeness is marred by sin, but it's not erased. "God values God's image . . . even if the likeness is blemished. . . . This is where we find our dignity . . . the worthiness we receive from God."[23] Christ proved your value by paying the ultimate price to redeem you. **Truth:** "God demonstrates God's love for us in this: While we were still sinners, Christ died for us" (Rom 5:8). You **are** worth Jesus to God: an infinite worth.
- **Identity in Christ:** When you trust in Jesus, your core identity changes. You aren't identified by your sin in God's eyes, but by Christ's righteousness. "Therefore, if anyone is in Christ, they are a new creation. The old has passed away; behold, the new has come" (2 Cor 5:17).[24] You are a renewed person, not "forever an addict." Yes, you may still struggle, but that struggle doesn't define you. God's grace does. **Truth:** "I'm a new creation in Christ. My past doesn't dictate my future; God's power and love do."
- **Forgiveness and cleansing:** No matter how great your sin, God's grace is greater. "Though your sins are like scarlet, they shall be as white as snow" (Isa 1:18). "As far as the east is from the west, so far has God removed our transgressions from us" (Ps 103:12). In Jesus, you have complete forgiveness (1 John 1:9). **Truth:** You aren't beyond hope: God can cleanse and pardon you. There's **no condemnation** for those in Christ (Rom 8:1).

Take time with these truths. Which ones are hardest for you to believe? Highlight those; often those are precisely where the enemy has been attacking your heart. **Challenge:** For the next one to two weeks, pick one truth to affirm each day (perhaps every morning). For example, stand in front of a mirror and say, "God delights in me and calls me God's child" (see Zeph 3:17, 1 John 3:1). It may feel awkward, but speak it as an act of faith. You are re-training your mind according to God's word, essentially "trying on" your true identity. Over time, as you persist, your feelings will begin to shift to align with God's reality. Remember, **your identity is in Christ now**,

22. Timmons, "Christian Faith-Based Recovery Theory."

23. Chandler, "Made in the Image of God."

24. Howard, "2 Corinthians 5:17 and Addiction Recovery."

not in your addiction or failures.[25] You are precious in God's sight (Isa 43:4). Let that sink in daily.

*If deep struggles persist in this area, consider working with a Christian counselor or mentor. Sometimes our image of God and self is tied to past wounds (like an abusive parent or trauma). Healing those memories with professional help can significantly enhance your ability to receive God's love. Don't hesitate to seek that help as an additional step.*

## Triggers and Temptations Map

### Purpose

A trigger is anything (emotional, situational, or relational) that tempts you to return to your addictive behavior. Identifying your triggers is a cornerstone of relapse prevention.[26] This tool helps you map out what leads you into temptation and, critically, to devise **spiritual and practical strategies** to respond. The Bible urges us to "be alert and of sober mind" (1 Pet 5:8): knowing your triggers keeps you alert. And God promises a "way of escape" for every temptation (1 Cor 10:13), which we'll plan for here. Essentially, you'll create a personal battle plan: "When X trigger occurs, I'll respond with Y (healthy coping or spiritual tool) instead of relapse."

### Instructions

Use the worksheet below to list your triggers in three categories. Then, for each trigger, write one or more interventions or coping strategies. Think of these interventions as the escape routes or holy strategies God provides to help you overcome. We've provided examples and ideas in each section.

### Identify Your Triggers

Self-awareness is key. Pray for insight and list anything that has caused cravings or slip-ups in the past.

- **Emotional triggers:** What feelings or internal states tend to drive you to use? Common ones are **H.A.L.T. (Hungry, Angry, Lonely, Tired)**,

25. Chandler, "Made in the Image of God."
26. S2L Recovery, "Faith-Based Relapse Prevention Strategies."

which make us vulnerable.[27] Others include boredom, stress/anxiety, depression/sadness, shame, excitement (even positive stress can trigger urges), or feeling overwhelmed. (Example entries: "When I feel rejected or lonely on a Friday night, I crave alcohol" or "When I get anxious about work, I want to use alcohol to relax"). List your top emotional danger zones. Be specific: "Feeling __________ leads me to want __________."

- **Situational triggers:** What external situations, places, or times spark your urges? Examples: Being around others who drink or use; specific social settings (parties, bars, concerts); unstructured time alone at night; payday (having extra cash); weekends; visiting a particular neighborhood; even specific music or seeing paraphernalia. Include routines associated with your acting out. (Example: "Driving past the liquor store on my way home" or "Being on my computer late at night triggers me to view pornography"). Write down any patterns you notice: people, places, things, or events that trigger you.[28]
- **Relational triggers:** Interactions and relationship dynamics can be triggers. Conflict or criticism might drive you to escape into using. Being around certain friends who enable or encourage substance use is a significant trigger. Social pressure or even gatherings (like family holidays) that stir up emotions can be risky. Also consider **negative influences**: anyone in your life who tends to drag you toward relapse. (Example: "When I fight with my spouse, I have the urge to get high to numb out," or "Hanging out with my old buddies from college usually ends with us getting drunk"). List any relational stressors or toxic relationships that trigger you.

## Strategize Your Interventions

For each trigger above, plan a coping strategy or preventative action. You might use a table with two columns (Trigger → My Coping Plan). Below are ideas to inspire you; choose the one that best suits you, and be specific.

- **Prayer and Scripture:** One of the most powerful immediate responses is to turn to prayer or recite Scripture when you feel tempted. As a faith-based strategy, "Watch and pray so that you won't fall into temptation" (Matt 26:41). You could carry a note card with a favorite verse

27. Bradford Health Services, "HALT."
28. S2L Recovery, "Faith-Based Relapse Prevention Strategies."

that empowers you (e.g., 1 Cor 10:13 or Phil 4:13) and read it out loud. Some make it a habit to pray the **Serenity Prayer** or a simple "Help me, Lord" in the heat of the moment. This invites God's strength in areas where you are weak.[29]

- **Escape the situation:** For situational triggers, often the best plan is **avoidance** or removal. Don't linger in tempting environments. Plan alternate routes to bypass that liquor store. If a particular hour of the day is perilous, schedule a healthy activity or avoid being alone during that time. If certain websites or apps are a problem, consider installing filters or removing access. Literally "flee" the trigger when possible (see 2 Tim 2:22: "Flee the evil desires of youth . . ."). There's no shame in steering clear of people or places that endanger your recovery: it's wisdom. Jesus said if your hand causes you to stumble, cut it off (Mark 9:43); in other words, take radical action to eliminate triggers.
- **Support network:** Identify who you can call or be with when a craving hits. Connection is the opposite of addiction. This could be a sponsor, an accountability partner, a close friend, or a member of a support group. Plan to call or text someone and **share your temptation**; often just talking about the urge weakens its power. Additionally, consider joining a recovery meeting, a Celebrate Recovery group, or a prayer group when you feel shaky. Sharing with others brings your struggle into the light, providing encouragement and accountability.[30]
- **Healthy distraction or coping skill:** Prepare a list of positive activities that help you ride the wave of craving. Cravings typically rise and fall like a wave; if you can occupy yourself for even twenty to thirty minutes, often the intensity passes. Ideas: go for a brisk walk or exercise (burn off anger or anxiety); take a shower; play music and sing; journal out your feelings; practice deep breathing or grounding techniques; work on a hobby; read a Psalm or uplifting book. Engage your mind and body in something constructive until the urge subsides. (For example, if loneliness is a trigger, your plan might be "When I feel lonely on a weekend, I'll immediately go to a coffee shop or call a friend to avoid isolation." If anger triggers you: "When I'm mad, I'll hit the gym or pray psalms rather than stew on it"). Have these strategies written down and easily accessible.

29. S2L Recovery, "Faith-Based Relapse Prevention Strategies."
30. S2L Recovery, "Faith-Based Relapse Prevention Strategies."

- **HALT self-care:** If you identified Hunger, Anger, Loneliness, or Tiredness as triggers, the antidote is to HALT and address that need.[31] If hungry, eat a healthy meal or snack (physical hunger can cloud judgment). If you're angry, use a constructive outlet (such as punching a pillow, doing a workout, or talking it through calmly later) and pray for calm. If lonely, reach out to someone or go where people are (don't trust the feeling that you must isolate; it's lying). If tired, rest! Take a nap or at least pause and relax. Many avoidable relapses happen simply because we let ourselves run on empty. Build regular rhythms of rest and replenishment. Remember, your body and mind are temples of God's Spirit (1 Cor 6:19); caring for them is a spiritual duty.

Write your specific plans next to each trigger on your list. For example: **Trigger:** "Friday after work, I drive by my old bar and feel like I deserve a drink." **Plan:** "Drive home a different way; once home, immediately go for a run or meet a friend for a movie. Text my accountability partner that I got through Friday sober." Make it as concrete as possible.

### Pray Over Your Trigger Plan

Commit your strategies to the Lord: "Lord, you know my weak moments. Strengthen me to follow these plans. When I'm tempted, remind me to seek you and the escape you provide.[32] Deliver me from evil, and lead me not into temptation (Matt 6:13). Amen." Keep this map somewhere visible (in your wallet, journal, or on the fridge) as a daily reminder that **temptations will come, but with God's help and wise planning, you aren't defenseless**.

## Recovery Identity Statement

### Purpose

The goal of this exercise is to help you articulate a new, biblically grounded identity for yourself, one that isn't defined by your addiction but by your relationship to Christ. In many recovery circles, people introduce themselves as "Hi, I'm ________ and I'm an addict." There's value in the honesty of admitting the struggle, but **your addiction isn't your ultimate identity**. Your worst sin or label doesn't define you; God's love and grace define you.

31. Bradford Health Services, "HALT."
32. S2L Recovery, "Faith-Based Relapse Prevention Strategies."

In Christ, you are a redeemed, beloved person with a hopeful future.[33] Research in faith-based recovery underscores that embracing a positive identity in Christ (child of God, new creation) fosters resilience and lasting change.[34] This exercise invites you to declare who you are, in God's eyes, and who you are becoming in recovery. It's like writing a mission statement for your new life.

## Instructions

Spend some time in prayer and reflection. Look back at the truths you've uncovered in prior exercises (especially the God/Self-Image Inventory). Then, write a short statement (a few sentences or a paragraph) that captures your identity in Christ and your commitment to recovery. This is personal; there's no formula. The key is that it's written in the affirmative, focusing on who you are (or are becoming) by God's grace, rather than what you're not. Think of it as planting a flag in the ground, declaring, "This is the real me, and by God's help, I'll live accordingly."

To help get started, consider these components for your statement (you can include all or just some):

- **Who you are in Christ:** e.g., a beloved son/daughter of God, forgiven and washed clean, a new creation, God's workmanship, temple of the Holy Spirit, heir to God's promises, etc. What identity word or phrase resonates most with you? (See Scriptures like 1 Pet 2:9, 1 John 3:1, Eph 2:10, 2 Cor 5:17.)
- **What you are called to:** e.g., free and sober, walking in the light, set apart for God's purpose, a living testimony of God's power, servant of others, etc. This links your identity to your purpose in recovery.
- **Your rejection of the old identity:** You might explicitly renounce the labels or lies of the past (e.g., "I'm not a slave to addiction; I'm free in Christ," or "I refuse the lie that I'm worthless; I'm precious to God"). This is optional, but can be powerful.
- **A Scripture or promise:** Including a favorite Bible verse can reinforce your statement (e.g., "I can do all things through Christ who gives me strength" Phil 4:13, or "God who began a good work in me will carry it to completion" Phil 1:6).

33. Howard, "2 Corinthians 5:17 and Addiction Recovery."
34. Timmons, "Christian Faith-Based Recovery Theory."

## Example Recovery Identity Statement

This is just one example. Yours should reflect your journey and voice.

> *"My past addictions don't define me: I'm a* **new creation in Christ; the old has gone, the new has come.**[35] *I'm a beloved child of God, forgiven and set free by the blood of Jesus. I'm called to live in freedom and truth, not in bondage or secrecy. With God's Spirit in me, I'm strong, loving, and self-controlled (2 Tim 1:7). My life has purpose: to glorify God and help others. I'm no longer a slave to fear or shame.* ***By the grace of God, I'm becoming whole****: one day at a time."*

## Make It Visible

Once you've written your identity statement, consider **making it visible**: put it on a card in your wallet, or stick it to your bathroom mirror. Read it every morning for the next thirty days. Let it remind you of **who you truly are**. When you stumble or have a bad day, use it as an opportunity to counteract negative self-talk. This isn't wishful thinking; it's aligning with God's declaration about you. "See what great love the Father has lavished on us, that we should be called children of God! **And that's what we are**" (1 John 3:1).

## Share It

Finally, **share it** if you can: with a trusted friend, mentor, or support group. Owning your new identity in front of others adds power and accountability. They can remind you of these words if you ever need to recall them. Remember, identity formation is a process. As you walk with Jesus, you'll grow increasingly into this true identity. Whenever the old labels or shame voices try to return, come back and read what you've written. **This is you now.** God says so, and God's word is final.

## Sources

These tools are informed by a blend of current addiction research and timeless biblical truth. Psychological models, such as the Stages of Change and

35. Howard, "2 Corinthians 5:17 and Addiction Recovery."

relapse prevention strategies, are integrated with spiritual principles of confession, renewal of the mind, and identity in Christ.[36] They draw on insights from trauma recovery (unmet needs fueling addiction), Christian counseling perspectives on shame and God's image, and faith-based recovery programs (e.g., Celebrate Recovery's emphasis on honesty and surrender).[37] By engaging both the head and the heart (combining clinical wisdom and biblical theology), these assessments aim to foster deep, shame-free self-reflection, leading to spiritual growth. Use them prayerfully, and may the Holy Spirit guide you into all truth and freedom as you work through each one. **"Then you will know the truth, and the truth will set you free"** (John 8:32).

## Sources and Resources


- Alcoholics Anonymous. *Alcoholics Anonymous*, 2001.
- Baker, *Life's Healing Choices*, 2007.
- Carnes, *Out of the Shadows*, 2001.
- Cloud and Townsend, *Boundaries*, 1992.
- DiClemente, *Addiction and Change*, 2006.
- Grim and Grim, "Belief, Behavior, and Belonging," 2019.
- Keller, *Counterfeit Gods*, 2009.
- Langberg, *Suffering and the Heart of God*, 2015.
- May, *Addiction and Grace*, 1988.
- Miller and Rollnick, *Motivational Interviewing*, 2013.
- Welch, *Addictions*, 2001.


36. Arista Recovery, "Stages of Change in Addiction Recovery"; Howard, "2 Corinthians 5:17 and Addiction Recovery"; S2L Recovery, "Faith-Based Relapse Prevention Strategies"; Timmons, "Christian Faith-Based Recovery Theory."

37. K., "Roots of Addiction"; Kelsey, "Celebrate Recovery Lesson One"; Chandler, "Made in the Image of God."

# Appendix E

# Tools for Sponsors, Mentors, and Support Groups

These seven tools are **group-friendly, Scripture-integrated resources** designed for mentoring relationships, spiritual direction, and small group support. They provide wisdom, grace, and structure to help sponsors, mentors, or support group leaders walk alongside others in recovery. Such peer support and mentorship have been shown to significantly reduce relapse rates by providing accountability, practical coping strategies, and emotional encouragement.[1] These tools can be used in contexts like Celebrate Recovery groups, church-based mentoring programs, or informal peer relationships. Each can be adapted into a fillable "workbook-style" page or handout, accompanied by guidance notes, so that sponsors and mentors can confidently introduce and guide others through each tool.

## Check-In Framework: *The Four Anchors*

This is a simple **weekly check-in template** for one-on-one sponsor/mentee meetings or group accountability check-ins. Often called the Four Anchors, it centers on four reflective questions that help a person *anchor* their week in honest self-examination and spiritual perspective.[2] The questions include:

1. Siegel, "Role of Peer Support and Mentorship."

2. See Vineyard USA, "Emotionally Focused"; Baker, *Stepping Out of Denial*; Mulholland, *Invitation to a Journey*; Calhoun, *Spiritual Disciplines Handbook*.

- **"How is your soul?"** Opening up about one's inner life and emotional/spiritual wellbeing.
- **"Where have you seen God at work this week?"** Noticing and celebrating God's presence or interventions, which cultivates gratitude and hope.
- **"What's been difficult, tempting, or painful?"** Honest sharing of struggles, triggers, or pain points from the week, bringing them into the light for support.
- **"What's your next faithful step?"** Identifying one concrete action step of obedience or recovery for the coming week (e.g., attending a meeting, making amends, avoiding a known trigger).

By covering soul care, gratitude, challenges, and forward steps, these four anchors provide a balanced snapshot of the mentee's journey each week.

## Mentor Guidance

Introduce this tool by explaining that regular heart checks keep us grounded. A sponsor can model vulnerability by answering first (e.g., "This week my soul is anxious, but I saw God at work when . . .," etc.), setting the tone of honest sharing. Listen attentively without judgment during the check-in, affirm positive observations of God's work, and gently probe or pray about the difficulties shared. Conclude by helping the person define a realistic "next step" and commit to following up on it next time. Consistently using the Four Anchors builds a rhythm of openness and growth in the mentor-mentee relationship. It ensures that each week the person is heard, spiritually encouraged, lovingly challenged regarding temptations, and supported in taking their next faithful step.

## The Three-Circles Tool: *Triggers, Lies, and Truth*

The Three Circles tool is a guided conversation and prayer framework for moments when someone stumbles or feels strong temptation. It helps the individual process what happened by reflecting on three key aspects of the incident: **the trigger, the lie, and the truth.** Draw three circles (or three columns on paper) and walk through these questions.

- **Circle 1—Trigger:** "What triggered me?" Describe the situation, feeling, or cue that set off the temptation or lapse. Was it an external trigger (a place, a person, a stressor) or an internal trigger (a mood like loneliness, anger, hunger, etc.)?
- **Circle 2—Lie:** "What lie did I believe?" Identify the false belief or voice of temptation that came with the trigger. For example: "I deserve this drink; I can't cope without using; No one cares, so why not?" Addiction often whispers deceptive thoughts and lies in these moments. Recognizing the specific lie is crucial; it shines a light on the core temptation or negative belief at play.
- **Circle 3—Truth:** "What's God's truth about me or this situation?" Counter the lie with a corresponding **truth from Scripture or recovery principles**. For example, against the lie "I'll never change," one might declare the truth "God says I can do all things through Christ who gives me strength" (Phil 4:13). If the lie was "No one cares about me," the truth could be "God will never leave me, and I have people who love me." Essentially, Circle 3 is about replacing the addictive or harmful thought with **God's perspective**: affirming forgiveness, love, purpose, and strength available to the person.

After identifying each circle, the mentor and mentee **pray through it**, thanking God for revealing the trigger and the lie, then renounce the lie and proclaim the chosen truth. This practice is grounded in the biblical principle of "taking every thought captive" and making it obedient to Christ (2 Cor 10:5). By consciously rejecting the lie and speaking God's truth, the individual can break the power of temptation and realign their mindset with sobriety.

## Mentor Guidance

Use this tool when a sponsee says, "I messed up" or "I'm struggling with craving X." First, ensure a safe, non-shaming atmosphere: commend them for bringing it up. Then guide them circle by circle. You might say, "Let's figure out what led up to this. What triggered you?" Write down or draw the trigger in circle one, then ask, "And what were the thoughts or excuses in your mind at that time?" Help them label those as lies lovingly (e.g., "I hear you saying you felt 'I've already failed, might as well keep using': that's a common **lie** that shame tells us."). Next, turn to God's truth: open a Bible together if handy, or recall a memory verse or affirmation that applies. Encourage the person to speak that truth out loud. Finally, pray together, asking God to **solidify the truth** in their heart and thanking God for God's grace. Over time, this three-circle process trains mentees to pause in the face of temptation, identify the lie versus God's truth, and choose a healthy response before relapse occurs.

## "S.T.A.R." Conversation Tool *(for Crises and Confession)*

**S.T.A.R.** is an acronym for a compassionate, structured response when someone in recovery has a crisis: for instance, if they relapse or confess a painful struggle or secret. In those delicate moments, a sponsor or group leader might feel unsure how to react. The S.T.A.R. framework provides a calm, grace-filled way to handle the situation in four steps.

- **S: Stop and create space.** Pause whatever agenda or reaction you had, and **give full attention**. Take a deep breath; resist any urge to panic or scold. If in person, perhaps step aside to a private, safe setting. This "stop" also means withholding immediate judgment. The goal is to make space for the struggler to share freely, sensing that "it's okay, I'm here for you; let's talk."
- **T: Tell the truth.** Invite the individual to express what happened and what they're feeling honestly. Encourage them that this is a safe zone to "get it all out." Listen actively and patiently. Let them speak without interruption, correction, or shame. This step echoes the biblical call to "confess your sins to each other and pray for each other so that you may be healed" (Jas 5:16). The act of truthful confession in a gracious environment is the first step toward healing.
- **A: Acknowledge God's presence (and grace).** After they've shared, gently acknowledge that **God is with you both** in this moment. This can be as simple as a short prayer together ("Lord, we invite you into this situation; we need your help here"), or an affirmation: "I know God still loves you, and I do too. God has not abandoned you." Bringing God's presence and grace into the conversation counters the person's shame with hope. Remember Gal 6:1: we're to restore someone who has fallen **with a spirit of gentleness**, watching that we remain humble. Acknowledge that relapse or sin is serious, but God's mercy and power to restore are greater.
- **R: Redirect gently to the following steps.** Once the person feels heard and grace has been affirmed, help redirect their focus toward **solutions and restoration**. Ask, "What do you think is the next right

thing to do?" or suggest a step: "Let's figure out how to get you back on track." This might include praying for forgiveness, formulating a plan to avoid the trigger next time, eliminating any remaining substance or temptation, or contacting a counselor/pastor if needed. Offer your continued support (for example, "I'll check in with you daily for a while," or "Let's attend an extra meeting together this week."). The tone here is gentle redirection, not heavy-handed instruction. You are guiding them from a place of setback toward hope and action: showing that relapse or failure isn't the end, just a moment to learn from and move forward.

Using S.T.A.R. prevents the common extremes of either reacting in anger/fear or, on the other end, brushing the issue under the rug. Instead, it leads with grace and truth hand in hand.

### Mentor Guidance:

Memorize or keep a note of "S-T-A-R" so it's available in the heat of the moment. When someone calls you in crisis or confesses something hard, silently remind yourself to Stop (stay calm, pray inwardly), then let them Tell the truth fully. After listening, Acknowledge God's presence: you might share a reassuring promise (for example, "God is near to the brokenhearted" or "God's grace is sufficient even now"). Finally, help them Redirect by brainstorming solutions together. Always conclude such conversations with prayer, asking God for forgiveness, guidance, and strength. This structured yet loving response reinforces that while there are consequences for mistakes, **grace and accountability go hand in hand**. The individual walks away feeling both heard and helped (not condemned), which is exactly how Jesus would restore someone (John 8:10–11). This approach fulfills the law of Christ by bearing one another's burdens in love while also gently guiding them back to the light (Gal 6:1–2).

## Accountability Covenant Template

An **Accountability Covenant** is a simple written agreement between a recovering person and their sponsor (or between members of a small group) that spells out mutual commitments. The process of writing and signing a covenant instills a sense of serious commitment to recovery and each other, under God's guidance. It's "official" enough to underscore the importance of accountability, yet personal and full of grace. A typical covenant document can be one page and include:

- **Weekly check-in commitment:** An agreement on meeting or talking **regularly (e.g., weekly)** for check-ins. It might specify the day/time or at least that both parties will make it a priority to connect and answer the Four Anchors questions honestly each week.
- **Specific areas of focus:** A list of the key areas or behaviors the mentee is working on. For example: sobriety from [substance/behavior], daily prayer or Bible reading, church attendance, truthful communication, etc. This section essentially says, "These are the areas I ask you to hold me accountable in." It gives the sponsor permission to ask about those areas. It can also include any particular boundaries ("I agree not to go to bars or to call you if I feel tempted to") or positive habits the person wants to maintain.
- **Emergency protocol (relapse/temptation plan):** A clear plan for what the mentee will do **in case of strong temptation or a slip/relapse**, and how the sponsor or group will respond. For instance, "If I feel close to relapsing, I'll text or call my sponsor immediately, day or night." And "If I relapse, I agree to inform my accountability partner within 24 hours and meet to discuss a plan of action." Likewise, the partner might commit, "If you call in crisis, I'll pray with you and come help if possible," or "If you disappear, I'll reach out and, if needed, alert [another support person]." Having a predefined response plan removes uncertainty and panic, ensuring both people know what to do if things get tough.[3]
- **Statement of mutual grace and commitment:** A closing paragraph in the covenant usually affirms that both parties are committed to honesty and grace. For example, "I, [name], commit to being truthful about my struggles and to accepting feedback/prayer. I understand my sponsor/mentor is here to help, not to judge me. I also acknowledge that slips may happen, and I agree not to hide them but to face them with honesty. In turn, I, [sponsor name], commit to maintaining confidentiality, offering support and guidance in love, and praying for you daily. We both rely on God's strength and grace in this journey." This kind of statement sets the tone that this is a **grace-based covenant**, not a legalistic contract. It reminds both people that accountability is about helping each other, not wielding power. You might include a verse like "Carry each other's burdens, and in this way you will fulfill the law of Christ" (Gal 6:2) right on the document to underscore this spirit.

3. Miranda, "Essential Components of a Relapse Prevention Plan."

Once the covenant is drafted, both the mentor and the mentee sign it and retain a copy for their records. Knowing you have this covenant provides clarity and reassurance. It's a gentle but firm reminder of the standards and supports in place. For the mentee, it serves almost like guardrails: They know, "If I get in trouble, here's what to do; I've promised to stay honest." For the sponsor, it serves as a reminder of their commitment to be available and supportive.

## Mentor Guidance

When introducing this tool, stress that the covenant isn't about punishment; it's about protection. It's making explicit the help and grace that are implicit in the relationship. Some mentors share their own experiences of how accountability was key in their recovery, emphasizing how "two are better than one" (Eccl 4:9–12 says a cord of three strands (you, me, and God) isn't easily broken). Work on the agreement together so it feels collaborative. Encourage the mentee to take the lead in drafting their areas of focus and triggers, thereby gaining ownership. As a sponsor, be clear about what you can commit to (for example, if you can't take calls at 3 a.m. due to family commitments, arrange for another backup support). Once signed, revisit the covenant occasionally (perhaps every few months) to check if any updates are needed or to celebrate that specific clauses (such as emergency calls) haven't been invoked. This document fosters trust: both parties are aware of the expectations, and there's a shared commitment to honesty and mutual understanding that can strengthen their relationship.

## Scripture and Prayer Deck

The Scripture and Prayer Deck is a **set of twenty to thirty cards**, each with a selected Bible verse (or short passage) on one side and a brief "breath prayer" or affirmation on the other. This tool brings the comfort and guidance of Scripture into group meetings or one-on-one time in an interactive way. It's beneficial when people aren't sure what to pray or need a quick dose of truth. Here are a few ways a deck can be used:

- **Opening or closing group meetings:** At the start or end of a support group session, pass the deck around and have each person draw a card at random. Please take a moment for each to read their verse aloud. This can lead to a time of reflection or a prayer inspired by the verses, much like popcorn-style prayer. Many find that the verse they "happened" to draw speaks directly to their current situation: a reminder that God's word is living and timely.

- **Random "verse draw" and discussion:** In a mentoring context, if a sponsee seems stuck or discouraged, you might shuffle the deck and invite them to draw a card. Read the verse together and ask, "What stands out to you in this verse?" or "How might this be speaking to what you're facing?" This can break the ice and initiate a spiritual conversation in a non-intimidating way, as the focus is on the verse. It also helps mentees learn to apply Scripture personally.
- **Crisis comfort:** Encourage individuals to carry a mini deck or a few favorite verse cards with them. In **moments of craving or anxiety**, when they might not have the words to pray, they can pull out a card, read the prayer and verse, and let that guide them. For example, a card might say on one side, "Psalm 46:1: God is our refuge and strength, an ever-present help in trouble." On the other side: "God, you are my refuge; help me through this moment." Breathing that prayer slowly can refocus someone's mind on God's power instead of the temptation.

Creating a Scripture deck can also be a group activity—writing out verses by hand on index cards or designing them on a computer to print and cut out. Aim for a mix of verses—some about God's **love and forgiveness** (for shame and guilt), some about **strength and escape from temptation** (for moments of weakness, e.g., 1 Cor 10:13), and others about **hope and identity in Christ**. Include a few short prayers like the Serenity Prayer or other affirmations that group members find meaningful.

## Mentor Guidance

When introducing the deck, explain the purpose: "Sometimes we don't know what to pray or say: these cards can help us find the words and remember God's promises." Share a personal anecdote if you have one (for instance, "I carried a card with Isaiah 41:10 for months; every time I felt like drinking, I'd read it and it gave me strength."). In group settings, be mindful of those new to faith or unfamiliar with the Bible; ensure to read the verses clearly and offer context if needed ("This was originally written to people in trouble, and it reminds us God is with us," etc.). The goal isn't to randomly magic a cure, but to foster **meditation on truth**. Over time, using the Scripture and Prayer Deck helps participants memorize key verses and teaches them to turn to prayer and God's word as a first resort in stress, rather than a last resort. It's a tangible way to hide God's word in their hearts and have it "on their lips" when needed (Ps 119:11, Josh 1:8).

## "Narrative Redemption" Testimony Workshop

This is a structured group activity or mentor/mentee exercise that guides individuals in **writing out their life testimony** (the story of their journey from addiction to healing) through three redemptive lenses. We call it Narrative Redemption because it helps them see God's redemptive hand at work in every chapter of their story. The process is usually broken into three parts (often written as three paragraphs or sections), with prompts for each:

- **Before—Life in Addiction:** Describe life before recovery or before encountering God's intervention. Who were you when you were in the depths of addiction or struggle? What was your daily life, mindset, and heart like? (E.g., "I was isolated, angry, and felt enslaved to alcohol. My life revolved around my next fix . . ."). This section is about being honest regarding the darkness and despair of the "before," so that the turnaround is clear. It shouldn't glorify the past, but it sets the stage by acknowledging the pain and hopelessness that were present.
- **Breakthrough—Encounter with God:** Describe the turning point or how **God intervened** to break the cycle. For many, this might include the moment of surrender or a cry for help, an experience in rehab or church, the influence of a loved one, etc. Essentially, how did you meet God (or hit bottom and become open to God) and what was that experience? (E.g., "In my lowest moment, I remembered the prayer of my youth and cried out to God . . . and God answered. I entered a recovery program where I learned that Christ's power could restore me . . ."). This is the pivot point where the story shifts from despair to hope. It highlights God's grace: whether through a scripture that spoke to them, a miraculously opened door, or simply the inner transformation of accepting help. Many testimony frameworks identify this as the moment you decided to change, and God gave you the strength to do so.[4]
- **Becoming—Who I'm Now:** Describe life after engaging in recovery and walking with God: the ongoing transformation. This isn't "I'm perfect now" but rather **who you are becoming** thanks to God's work. Focus on the positive changes and healing: freedom from certain chains, restored relationships, new purpose, etc. (E.g., "Now, by God's grace,

4. Masters, "Write a Powerful Testimony."

I'm two years sober. I wake up with hope and purpose. I'm reconciling with my family, and helping others who struggle with the same things I did . . ."). It's powerful here to include what you've learned and how God is using your story now. This section should radiate hope, showing that **change is possible** and ongoing. As one recovery testimony guideline puts it, share "how Christ is changing your life today and the hope you have for the future."[5]

After writing these three parts, the workshop often includes time for **sharing** (if the person is willing) or, at the very least, reflection. Sharing a testimony in a group can be incredibly encouraging for both the speaker and the listeners: it says, "God brought me through; God can do it for you too." However, it's stressed that sharing is voluntary and should be done with some guidelines for safety, humility, and hope. **Safety** means not divulging details that could trigger others or hurt people who might be mentioned in the story (e.g., it's wise to avoid graphic descriptions of using or to keep others anonymous). **Humility** means the story should ultimately glorify God's grace, not the person or the sin, avoiding any sense of bragging about "how bad I was" or focusing excessively on the past. **Hope** means ending with God's redeeming work and the positive path forward, so that those who hear it are left uplifted, not depressed. A facilitator or sponsor can provide tips such as keeping it to five to ten minutes, focusing more on the change than the mess, and perhaps practicing beforehand. In some cases, it's helpful to have the mentor **review** the written testimony and provide gentle feedback, ensuring the tone is redemptive and that no confidential information about third parties is accidentally revealed.

## Mentor Guidance

Frame this activity by referencing the idea that "God turns our mess into a message." Many people in recovery feel shame about their past; writing it out as a testimony helps break the power of that shame and reframe their experiences as a source of encouragement to others.[6] If doing this one-on-one, you, as the mentor, might first share your testimony in the Before/Breakthrough/Becoming format to provide a live example. In a group workshop, give a handout with the three section prompts and maybe a couple of key questions for each to get them thinking (for instance, "Before: What were you like? What was your lowest point? What false beliefs kept you in

5. Masters, "Write a Powerful Testimony."
6. Masters, "Write a Powerful Testimony."

bondage? . . . Breakthrough: How did you realize you needed God? How did you accept Christ or decide to change? . . . Becoming: What are the biggest changes in your life? What hope would you offer someone else?"). Give people time (maybe over a week or two) to write their story. Then, create a safe meeting where those who want to share can do so. Often, this is a sacred time: tears, laughter, hugs, and a profound sense of God's presence as each story testifies to **God's redeeming power**. Emphasize that even if someone chooses not to share publicly, the act of writing it for themselves is still valuable; it's an Ebenezer (stone of remembrance) of how far they've come. Encourage keeping that written testimony in a special place, and updating it as the journey continues. The Narrative Redemption tool helps individuals see purpose in their pain and recognize their personal story as part of God's larger story of redemption.

## Relapse Response Plan

A Relapse Response Plan is a prepared, **grace-filled action plan** for how to respond if a relapse occurs (or if someone comes very close to relapse). It's sometimes called an "after-action plan" or an "emergency relapse plan." The idea is to prevent a full-blown spiral by having a concrete set of steps to take immediately after a slip, when emotions like shame, guilt, or fear are most likely to drive a person back into hiding. By deciding these steps ahead of time, the person can move quickly from "I messed up" to "I'm getting back on track." Key components often include:

- **A brief reflection worksheet.** This is a one-page guide with questions to help you calmly analyze the relapse. It might ask, "When did it happen, and what led up to it? What was the trigger? How were you feeling? What can you learn from this experience?" Writing down the answers (or discussing them with a mentor) helps the individual view the relapse as **data for growth** rather than an excuse for self-condemnation. It turns the event into an opportunity to better understand vulnerabilities. Some worksheets also include affirmations, such as "I'm still God's beloved child," to remind the person not to identify with the failure.
- **Scriptures of grace and restoration.** A small list of three to five go-to Bible verses that speak of God's forgiveness, grace, and ability to restore. When someone has fallen, their mind is often full of negative self-talk ("I blew it, I'm hopeless"). Replacing that with **God's word** is critical. Examples: "There is now no condemnation for those who are

in Christ Jesus" (Rom 8:1), "Though the righteous fall seven times, they rise again" (Prov 24:16), "If we confess our sins, God is faithful to forgive and cleanse us" (1 John 1:9), or Ps 51. These verses can be printed on the plan or kept on note cards. The person should read them out loud to let the truth start to wash away the shame. This reinforces that God hasn't given up on them.

- **Prayer of recommitment.** A written sample prayer (or one the person composes themselves when sober) to pray after a relapse. For instance: "Creator God, I'm sorry I gave in to temptation. Thank you for your mercy that's new every morning. I receive your forgiveness through Christ. I ask for strength to start again right now. Please help me learn from my mistakes and move forward with honesty and humility. I recommit myself to your care and my recovery. In Jesus's name, Amen." Saying a prayer like this helps break the isolation and self-hatred that try to settle in after a fall. It's essentially leading the person straight back into connection with God, rather than allowing a relapse to drive a wedge.
- **Phone tree or support contact list.** The plan should list **who to call immediately**, ideally several people in order: e.g., 1) Call my sponsor (insert name/number); 2) If they're not reachable, call my accountability partner or a supportive friend (name/number); 3) If I feel unsafe or in danger of continuing to use, call a crisis line or check into [rehab/support center]. This removes guesswork. The moment a relapse happens, the instruction is: pick up the plan and start at step 1 on the list. Many people hesitate to reach out due to shame, so the plan pre-commits them: "I have promised to call, and my support people have agreed to be there for me." Likewise, sponsors should have a copy of this plan; if they receive that call, they'll know this is part of the agreed-upon response and react calmly and helpfully (perhaps coming over to be with the person or taking them to a meeting, depending on the scenario).

Overall, the Relapse Response Plan is about **bouncing back quickly with grace**. Instead of a relapse leading to "might as well give up" thinking, it becomes a trigger for an immediate increase in support and self-care. Research in addiction recovery underscores that having a predetermined plan for lapses greatly improves long-term outcomes, because it interrupts the cycle of shame and hiding that can turn a single lapse into a prolonged bender.[7]

7. Miranda, "Essential Components of a Relapse Prevention Plan"; AToN Center, "High-Risk Situations for Relapse."

### Mentor Guidance

Develop this plan **proactively** with your sponsee, preferably early on, when they're clear-headed and committed to recovery. Emphasize that this isn't expecting relapse, but being wisely prepared "just in case," much like having a fire escape plan. This can reduce fear of the unknown. When walking through the plan, discuss each element: "Which verses speak to you? Who are three people you absolutely must call if you slip?" Ensure the individual genuinely agrees and feels comfortable with the steps. Remind them that calling you (or others) after a relapse is about getting help, not getting scolded. Affirm that **nothing they do will make you love them less**: the plan is there to prove that. In the emotional aftermath of a relapse, a person may not trust their mind; having the plan to hold physically and follow is grounding. If a relapse occurs, as a mentor, follow through on your end: respond with love, meet up as soon as possible to complete the reflection worksheet together, pray with them, and help reinforce that this is a setback, not the end. Afterward, encourage tweaking the Recovery Plan if needed (maybe there are new safeguards to put in place or a new trigger identified). Also, celebrate the fact that they pulled out the plan and used it! That itself is a victory and a sign of growth. In summary, the Relapse Response Plan transforms what could be a moment of total defeat into a **platform for grace** ("get back up," as Scripture says) and learning.[8] This way, even falls are redeemed as part of the recovery journey, and no one must stay stuck in the shame of yesterday's mistake.

## Conclusion

Using tools like these, sponsors and support group leaders can foster a structured yet caring environment for recovery. They provide practical handles for discipleship and accountability, while keeping God's redemptive truth at the center. By integrating check-ins, guided conversations, covenants, Scripture, personal storytelling, and emergency plans, a mentor can confidently say, "Let's walk this road together." Each tool is a means of extending the hope, grace, and wisdom that lead to lasting freedom. Together, as the Body of Christ supporting one another, no one must fight their battle alone and that makes all the difference.[9]

8. Anchored Tides Recovery, "Relapse Definition in Addiction."
9. Siegel, "Role of Peer Support and Mentorship."

# Appendix F

# Scripture Meditations and Prayers for Recovery

## Psalm 51—a Prayer of Repentance

There are moments in recovery when guilt rises like a tide, threatening to drown the fragile seeds of hope. In those moments, Ps 51 becomes a lifeline. Born from David's broken heart after his moral failure, this psalm gives voice to our longing for mercy and our ache for inner renewal. "Have mercy on me, O God, according to your unfailing love . . ." This isn't the cry of someone excusing their behavior. It's the raw plea of a soul finally done with pretending. When we meditate on this psalm, we're invited into a sacred honesty, a chance to name our failures not with shame, but with trust in divine mercy.

The words "Create in me a pure heart, O God, and renew a steadfast spirit within me" (Ps 51:10) are a gentle yet powerful petition for inner reformation. Not just a patch-up job, but a new creation. In recovery, we're not asking to return to who we were; we're asking to become someone new, formed in mercy, steadied by grace.

Let this psalm be your companion when you feel the weight of your past pressing in. Let it guide your prayer when you've slipped or stumbled. Pray it not just as David's lament but as your own: "Wash me, and I shall be whiter than snow." These aren't just poetic words; they're the lived hope that guilt can give way to joy, and confession can open the door to freedom. God doesn't despise a broken spirit; God heals it.

## Isaiah 61:1–3—Promise of Freedom and Restoration

The language of Isa 61 is balm for the weary and gospel for the addicted. These verses echo across centuries with the same thunderous hope: God comes to set the captives free. "To bind up the brokenhearted . . . to proclaim liberty to the captives . . . to comfort all who mourn." This is no vague spiritual comfort; it's a mission statement, a declaration of divine intent, fulfilled in Jesus and extended now to all who live in chains of sorrow, shame, or addiction.

When you read Isa 61:1–3 slowly and prayerfully, you'll begin to hear your name in its promise. This passage doesn't speak of freedom as theory; it proclaims it as your inheritance. The God who anointed the Messiah to bring liberty still speaks freedom over your life today. God trades ashes for beauty, mourning for oil of gladness, despair for garments of praise. This isn't mere sentiment. It's a transformation.

Use these verses as a prayer: "Lord, bind up my broken heart. Release me from the prison I've built. Plant in me hope instead of despair." Each time you speak these words, let them root deeper into your spirit. Let them become a banner over your recovery journey: God's dream for you isn't just sobriety, but wholeness. Not just survival, but joy. And not just an end to captivity, but the rising of a new life, firmly planted like oaks of righteousness in the garden of grace.

## Matthew 11:28–30—Rest for the Weary

Addiction is a taskmaster that never relents. It demands more, gives less, and finally leaves us hollow. Jesus offers a different kind of yoke, not one that tightens and strangles but one that fits gently, offering rest. "Come to me, all you who are weary and burdened, and I'll give you rest." These aren't words for the strong and self-sufficient. They are a summons for the tired, the bruised, the overwhelmed, those who have tried to carry life's weight on their own and found themselves crushed beneath it.

In recovery, this invitation becomes a sacred breath. It reminds us that we don't need to prove ourselves worthy of divine love; we're invited to come. Jesus doesn't scold or shame. He calls. He offers rest, not as a fleeting feeling but as a deep unburdening of the soul.

Take time to pray these verses slowly, one phrase at a time. "Come to me . . ." Imagine yourself doing just that. "My yoke is easy. . ." Imagine trading your burden for the weight of grace. "You will find rest . . ." Not just for your body, but for your soul.

Whenever temptation creeps in, or shame returns, or exhaustion sets in: return to this invitation. Let it quiet your mind. Let it speak over your inner turmoil. Jesus's yoke isn't a new burden; it's the strength to walk in step with One who carries what you can't. In Christ, there is rest that heals, restores, and renews.

## 1 Corinthians 10:13—a Way Out of Temptation

There's a lie that often hisses in the ears of the recovering: "You can't help it. You'll always be this way. There's no way out." But Scripture confronts that lie with fierce truth. "No temptation has overtaken you except what's common to humanity. And God is faithful . . ." These words don't deny the reality of struggle. They name it and then flood it with hope. Temptation is real but so is God's faithfulness.

This verse doesn't promise a life free from temptation. It promises something better: endurance, strength, and a path forward. "God . . . won't let you be tempted beyond what you can bear. But . . . will provide a way out so that you can endure it." This is the kind of promise to carry in your pocket, to speak aloud when cravings rise, to cling to when escape feels impossible.

When tempted, don't just grit your teeth. Pause. Breathe. Pray: "God, where is the way out?" It might be a call to a friend. A walk around the block. A psalm whispered aloud. A moment of remembering who you are and whose you are. God's way out is often quieter than the craving, but it's always present.

Meditating on this verse builds spiritual muscle. It shifts the posture of the heart from defeat to expectation: God will meet me here. God will show me a path. I'm not alone. The next time temptation comes knocking, don't panic, look for the door God has already cracked open.

## The Serenity Prayer—Living Surrender Daily

Few words have held so many souls in recovery as the Serenity Prayer.[1] Though not found in Scripture, it sings in harmony with biblical wisdom. "God, grant me the serenity to accept the things I can't change . . ." This is the prayer of surrender; the realization that not everything is in our control and that peace is found not in managing everything but in releasing what we can't.

1. Niebuhr, *Serenity Prayer.*

"Courage to change the things I can . . ." This is the cry of agency, of recognizing that grace doesn't render us passive. We're invited to co-labor with God, to participate in our healing. Courage is required because change is painful. Recovery demands choices, boundaries, and brave steps.

"And wisdom to know the difference." This final line is the hinge. Wisdom is the gift that discerns when to act and when to wait. When to speak and when to stay silent. When to push and when to release. James 1:5 reminds us that God gives wisdom generously to those who ask for it.

This prayer, prayed daily (morning and night, in silence or aloud) can become a rhythm of grace. In anxious moments, speak it slowly. In moments of doubt, let it realign your spirit. Over time, these words begin to form the spine of a surrendered life: one grounded in trust, humility, courage, and spiritual clarity.

The Serenity Prayer isn't a magic spell. It's a lived posture. A way of breathing when the air feels tight. A way of trusting when control slips. A way of walking hand-in-hand with grace.

# About the Author

Graham Joseph Hill (OAM, PhD) is an Adjunct Research Fellow and Associate Professor at Charles Sturt University and one of Australia's most prolific and awarded Christian authors. He's written more than twenty books, including *Salt, Light, and a City*, which was named Jesus Creed's 2012 Book of the Year (church category); *Healing Our Broken Humanity* (with Grace Ji-Sun Kim), named Outreach Magazine's 2019 Resource of the Year (culture category); and *World Christianity*, shortlisted for the 2025 Australian Christian Book of the Year. In 2024, Graham was awarded the Medal of the Order of Australia (OAM) for his service to theological education. He lives in Sydney with his wife Shyn.

See Graham's author website and Substack:
grahamjosephhill.com
grahamjosephhill.substack.com

# Bibliography

Akanbi, Maxwell O., et al. "A Systematic Review of the Effectiveness of Employer-Led Interventions for Drug Misuse." *Journal of Occupational Health* 62 (2020) e12133.

Alcoholics Anonymous. *Alcoholics Anonymous: The Story of How Many Thousands of Men and Women Have Recovered from Alcoholism.* New York: Alcoholics Anonymous World Services, 2001.

———. *Twelve Steps and Twelve Traditions.* New York: Alcoholics Anonymous World Services, 1952.

Anchored Tides Recovery. "Relapse Definition in Addiction." Anchored Tides Recovery, February 17, 2025. https://anchoredtidesrecovery.com/relapse-definition-part-of-the-addiction-cycle/.

Anderson, Neil T. *The Bondage Breaker: Overcoming Negative Thoughts, Irrational Feelings, and Habitual Sins.* Eugene, OR: Harvest House, 2000.

Arista Recovery. "The Stages of Change in Addiction Recovery." Arista Recovery, July 10, 2025. https://www.aristarecovery.com/blog/stages-of-change/.

Arms Acres. "5 Common Fears in Recovery and How to Overcome Them." Arms Acres, April 4, 2024. https://www.armsacres.com/blog/fears-in-recovery.

Arterburn, Stephen, and David Stoop, eds. *The Life Recovery Bible: New Living Translation.* Carol Stream, IL: Tyndale, 2017.

AToN Center. "High-Risk Situations for Relapse and How to Avoid Them." AToN Center, January 24, 2025. https://atoncenter.com/high-risk-situations-for-relapse/.

Augustine. *The City of God Against the Pagans.* Translated by R. W. Dyson. Cambridge: Cambridge University Press, 1998.

———. *Confessions.* Translated by Henry Chadwick. Oxford: Oxford University Press, 2008.

Baker, John. *Celebrate Recovery Leader's Guide: A Recovery Program Based on Eight Principles from the Beatitudes.* Grand Rapids: Zondervan, 2016.

———. *Celebrate Recovery Participant's Guides 1–4.* Grand Rapids: Zondervan, 2005.

———. *Life's Healing Choices: Freedom from Your Hurts, Hang-Ups, and Habits.* Nashville: Howard, 2007.

———. *Stepping Out of Denial Into God's Grace: Participant Guide 1.* Grand Rapids: Zondervan, 2005.

Betts, Anna. "US Gambling Firms Fight Protections Meant to Reduce Addiction-Related Harms, Watchdog Warns." *The Guardian*, April 15, 2025. https://www.theguardian.com/us-news/2025/apr/15/betting-firms-regulations.

Bonhoeffer, Dietrich. *Life Together*. New York: Harper & Row, 1954.

Bowen, Sarah, et al., *Mindfulness-Based Relapse Prevention for Addictive Behaviors: A Clinician's Guide*. New York: Guilford, 2021.

Bradford Health Services. "HALT: The Dangers of Hunger, Anger, Loneliness, and Tiredness." Bradford Health Services. https://bradfordhealth.com/halt-hunger-anger-loneliness-tiredness/.

Brueggemann, Walter. *The Prophetic Imagination*. 2nd ed. Minneapolis: Fortress, 2001.

Calhoun, Adele Ahlberg. *Spiritual Disciplines Handbook; Practices That Transform Us*. Downers Grove, IL: InterVarsity, 2015.

Calvin, John. *Institutes of the Christian Religion*. Translated by Ford Lewis Battles. Louisville: Westminster John Knox, 2006.

Carnes, Patrick J. *Out of the Shadows: Understanding Sexual Addiction*. 3rd ed. Center City, MN: Hazelden, 2001.

Cavanaugh, William T. *Being Consumed: Economics and Christian Desire*. Grand Rapids: Eerdmans, 2008.

Chandler, Chris. "Made in the Image of God: Learn to Feel Lovable with Christian Counseling." Bellevue Christian Counseling, October 29, 2013. https://bellevuechristiancounseling.com/articles/made-in-the-image-of-god-learn-to-feel-lovable-with-christian-counseling.

Changes Addiction Rehab. "The 12 Patterns of Denial and Rationalizing in Addiction." Changes Addiction Rehab. https://changesrehab.co.za/rationalising-in-addiction/.

Chapman, Gary, and Jennifer Thomas. *The Five Languages of Apology: How to Experience Healing in All Your Relationships*. Chicago: Northfield, 2006.

Claiborne, Shane, and Chris Haw. *Jesus for President: Politics for Ordinary Radicals*. Grand Rapids: Zondervan, 2008.

Cloud, Henry, and John Townsend. *Boundaries: When to Say Yes, How to Say No to Take Control of Your Life*. Grand Rapids: Zondervan, 1992.

Collins, Gary R. *Christian Counseling: A Comprehensive Guide*. 3rd ed. Nashville: Thomas Nelson, 2007.

Comer, John Mark. *Live No Lies: Recognize and Resist the Three Enemies That Sabotage Your Peace*. Colorado Springs: WaterBrook, 2021.

Dawn, Marva J. *A Royal Waste of Time: The Splendor of Worshiping God and Being Church for the World*. Grand Rapids: Eerdmans, 1999.

DiClemente, Carlo C. *Addiction and Change: How Addictions Develop and Addicted People Recover*. New York: Guilford, 2006.

El Hayek, Samer, et al. "Stigma Toward Substance Use Disorders: A Multinational Perspective." *Frontiers in Psychiatry* 15, February 1, 2024. https://www.frontiersin.org/journals/psychiatry/articles/10.3389/fpsyt.2024.1295818/full.

Emmons, Robert A. *Thanks! How Practicing Gratitude Can Make You Happier*. Boston: Houghton Mifflin Harcourt, 2007.

Foster, Richard J. *Celebration of Discipline: The Path to Spiritual Growth*. 3rd ed. San Francisco: HarperSanFrancisco, 1998.

Giesbrecht, et al. "The Impacts of Alcohol Marketing and Advertising, and the Alcohol Industry's Views on Marketing Regulations: Systematic Reviews of Systematic Reviews." *Drug Alcohol Rev.* 43 (2024) 1402–25.

Godkhindi, Parnika, et al. "They're Causing More Harm Than Good: A Qualitative Study Exploring Racism in Harm Reduction Through the Experiences of Racialized People Who Use Drugs." *Harm Reduction Journal* 19 (2022). https://harmreductionjournal.biomedcentral.com/articles/10.1186/s12954-22-00672-y.

Grim, Brian J., and Melissa E. Grim. "Belief, Behavior, and Belonging: How Faith is Indispensable in Preventing and Recovering from Substance Abuse." *Journal of Religion and Health* 58 (2019) 1713–50. https://pmc.ncbi.nlm.nih.gov/articles/PMC6759672/.

Grinspoon, Peter. "Poverty, Homelessness, and Social Stigma Make Addiction More Deadly." *Harvard Health*, September 28, 2021. https://www.health.harvard.edu/blog/poverty-homelessness-and-social-stigma-make-addiction-more-deadly-202109282602.

Hauerwas, Stanley, and William H. Willimon. *Resident Aliens: Life in the Christian Colony*. Nashville: Abingdon, 1989.

Haugk, Kenneth C. *Christian Caregiving: A Way of Life*. Minneapolis: Augsburg Fortress, 1984.

Hays, Richard B. *The Moral Vision of the New Testament*. San Francisco: HarperOne, 1996.

Hazelden Betty Ford Foundation. "The Twelve Steps of Alcoholics Anonymous." Hazelden Betty Ford Foundation, March 20, 2019. https://www.hazeldenbettyford.org/articles/twelve-steps-of-alcoholics-anonymous.

Howard, Patricia. "2 Corinthians 5:17 and Addiction Recovery: Embracing a New Identity in Christ." Detox to Rehab, April 18, 2025. https://detoxtorehab.com/christian/2-corinthians-5-17-new-identity-addiction.

Ignatius of Loyola. *Spiritual Exercises*. Christian Classics Ethereal Library. https://ccel.org/ccel/ignatius/exercises/exercises.

K., Steve. "The Roots of Addiction: Unmet Needs for Love and Security." 12-Step Philosophy, August 17, 2016. https://12stepphilosophy.org/2016/08/17/the-roots-of-addiction-unmet-needs-for-love-and-security.

Keller, Timothy. *Counterfeit Gods: The Empty Promises of Money, Sex, and Power, and the Only Hope That Matters*. New York: Dutton, 2009.

Kelsey, Michele L. "Celebrate Recovery Lesson 1: Denial." Sharing Life and Love. https://sharinglifeandlove.com/blog/celebrate-recovery-lesson-1-denial/.

Kim, Bokyung, et al. "The Opioid Crisis and the Role of Employers." Sanford Institute for Economic Policy Research, January 2024. https://siepr.stanford.edu/publications/policy-brief/opioid-crisis-and-role-employers.

Kittel, Gerhard, and Gerhard Friedrich, eds. *Theological Dictionary of the New Testament*. Translated by Geoffrey W. Bromiley. Grand Rapids: Eerdmans, 1964.

Kiwi Recovery. "Overcoming Substance Use, Abuse, and Chemical Dependency." Kiwi Recovery, April 9, 2025. https://www.kiwirecovery.com/addiction-treatment-blog/substance-use-abuse-and-chemical-dependency.

Koh, Howard. "What Led to the Opioid Crisis—and How to Fix It." Harvard T. H. Chan School of Public Health, February 9, 2022. https://hsph.harvard.edu/news/what-led-to-the-opioid-crisis-and-how-to-fix-it/.

Kraft, Charles H. *Defeating Dark Angels: Breaking Demonic Oppression in the Believer's Life*. Ann Arbor: Vine, 1992.

Langberg, Diane. *Suffering and the Heart of God: How Trauma Destroys and Christ Restores*. Greensboro: New Growth, 2015.

Leon Tesani, Rusette de. "How Stigma Affects Patients Seeking Help for Drug Addiction." *World Journal of Nursing Research* 4 (2025) 31–46.

Lin, Chunqing, et al. "A Scoping Review of Social Determinants of Health's Impact on Substance Use Disorders Over the Life Course." *Journal of Substance Abuse Treatment* 166 (2024) 209484. https://www.jsatjournal.com/article/S2949-8759%2824%2900196-96/fulltext.

Luther, Martin. "Lectures on Galatians." In *Luther's Works*, edited by Jaroslav Pelikan, 26:1–461. St. Louis: Concordia, 1963.

Marshall, Christopher D. *Beyond Retribution: A New Testament Vision for Justice, Crime, and Punishment*. Grand Rapids: Eerdmans, 2001.

Masters, Joshua J. "Write a Powerful Testimony Using These 5 Elements." The Write Conversation, September 10, 2021. https://thewriteconversation.blogspot.com/2021/09/write-powerful-testimony-using-these-5.html.

Maté, Gabor. *In the Realm of Hungry Ghosts: Close Encounters with Addiction*. Berkeley: North Atlantic, 2010.

May, Gerald G. *Addiction and Grace: Love and Spirituality in the Healing of Addictions*. San Francisco: HarperOne, 1988.

Mayo Clinic Staff. "Forgiveness: Letting Go of Grudges and Bitterness." Mayo Clinic, November 22, 2022. https://www.mayoclinic.org/healthy-lifestyle/adult-health/in-depth/forgiveness/art-20047692.

Merrefield, Clark. "Mental Health Care at Work: Roundup of Recent Research on Employee Assistance Programs." The Journalist's Resource, May 24, 2022. https://journalistsresource.org/health/employee-assistance-programs-mental-health/.

Miller, William R., and Stephen Rollnick. *Motivational Interviewing: Helping People Change*. 3rd ed. New York: Guilford, 2013.

Miranda, Matt. "Essential Components of a Relapse Prevention Plan." Restoration Recovery Center, June 17, 2024. https://restorationrecoverycenter.com/2024/06/17/essential-components-of-a-relapse-prevention-plan/.

Moltmann, Jürgen. *Theology of Hope: On the Ground and the Implications of a Christian Eschatology*. Minneapolis: Fortress, 1993.

Mulholland, M. Robert, Jr. *Invitation to a Journey: A Road Map for Spiritual Formation*. Downers Grove, IL: InterVarsity, 1993.

National Council on Problem Gambling, "Gambling Addiction Recovery, Investment, and Treatment (GRIT) Act." NCPG, 2025. https://www.ncpgambling.org/advocacy/grit-act/.

National Safety Council. *Substance Use and Stigma: Considerations for Employers*. NSC, March 29, 2021. https://www.nsc.org/safety-first/substance-use-and-stigma-considerations-for-employ.

Neff, Kristin. *Self-Compassion: The Proven Power of Being Kind to Yourself*. New York: William Morrow, 2015.

Niebuhr, Reinhold. *The Serenity Prayer*. In *Reinhold Niebuhr: Major Works on Religion and Politics*, edited by Elisabeth Sifton, 681. New York: Library of America, 2015.

Nouwen, Henri J. M. *The Inner Voice of Love: A Journey Through Anguish to Freedom*. New York: Doubleday, 1996.

———. *Life of the Beloved: Spiritual Living in a Secular World*. New York: Crossroad, 1992.

———. *The Wounded Healer: Ministry in Contemporary Society*. New York: Image, 1979.

Palmer, Parker J. *Let Your Life Speak: Listening for the Voice of Vocation*. San Francisco: Jossey-Bass, 2000.

Rehman, Maham, et al. "Structural Stigma Within Inpatient Care for People Who Inject Drugs: Implications for Harm Reduction." *Harm Reduction Journal* 21 (2024). https://harmreductionjournal.biomedcentral.com/articles/10.1186/s12954-24-00971-76.

Riccardi, Mike. "Augustine and Christian Longing." The Master's Seminary, February 28, 2020. https://blog.tms.edu/augustine-christian-longing.

Rohr, Richard. *Breathing Under Water: Spirituality and the Twelve Steps*. Cincinnati: Franciscan Media, 2011.

*The Rule of St. Benedict*. The Order of Saint Benedict. https://archive.osb.org/rb/text/toc.html.

Rundle, Samantha, et al. "Examining the Relationship Between Public Stigma, Models of Addiction, and Addictive Disorders." *Addiction Research and Theory* 33 (2024) 1–7. https://www.researchgate.net/profile/Samantha-Rundle-2/publication/381629693_Examining_the_relationship_between_public_stigma_models_of_addiction_and_addictive_disorders/links/66ec33a997a75a4b48365505/Examining-the-relationship-between-public-stigma-models-of-addiction-and-addictive-disorders.pdf.

S2L Recovery. "Faith-Based Relapse Prevention Strategies." S2L Recovery. https://www.s2lrecovery.org/faith-based-relapse-prevention-strategies.

Samba Recovery. "The Impact of Addiction on Spiritual Well-Being: Understanding the Spiritual Toll of Addiction." Samba Recovery, January 29, 2025. https://www.sambarecovery.com/rehab-blog/the-impact-of-addiction-on-spiritual-well-being.

Sande, Ken. *The Peacemaker: A Biblical Guide to Resolving Personal Conflict*. Grand Rapids: Baker, 2004.

Schmemann, Alexander. *For the Life of the World: Sacraments and Orthodoxy*. Crestwood, NY: St. Vladimir's Seminary, 1973.

Schwartz, Jeffrey M., and Rebecca Gladding. *You Are Not Your Brain: The 4-Step Solution for Changing Bad Habits, Ending Unhealthy Thinking, and Taking Control of Your Life*. New York: Avery, 2015.

Siegel, Adam. "The Role of Peer Support and Mentorship in Addiction Recovery." Olympic Behavioral Health, July 8, 2024. https://olympicbehavioralhealth.com/rehab-blog/peer-support-and-mentorship-in-addiction-recovery.

Smedes, Lewis B. *Forgive and Forget: Healing the Hurts We Don't Deserve*. San Francisco: HarperOne, 1984.

Smith, James K. A. *Desiring the Kingdom: Worship, Worldview, and Cultural Formation*. Grand Rapids: Baker Academic, 2009.

Substance Abuse and Mental Health Services Administration. *Medications for Opioid Use Disorder: Treatment Improvement Protocol (TIP) Series 63*. HHS Publication No. (SMA) 21–5063. Rockville: SAMHSA, 2021. https://library.samhsa.gov/sites/default/files/pep21-22-01-02.pdf.

———. *Trauma-Informed Care in Behavioral Health Services*. Treatment Improvement Protocol (TIP) Series 57. HHS Publication No. (SMA) 13–4801. Rockville: SAMHSA, 2014. https://library.samhsa.gov/sites/default/files/sma14-4816.pdf.

Thompson, Curt. *The Soul of Shame: Retelling the Stories We Believe About Ourselves*. Downers Grove, IL: InterVarsity, 2015.

Timmons, Shirley M. "A Christian Faith-Based Recovery Theory: Understanding God as Sponsor." Journal of Religion and Health 51 (2012) 1152–64.

Tutu, Desmond. *No Future Without Forgiveness*. New York: Image, 2000.

Tutu, Desmond, and Mpho Tutu. *The Book of Forgiving: The Fourfold Path for Healing Ourselves and Our World*. New York: HarperOne, 2014.

Tyndall, Mark, and Zoë Dodd. "How Structural Violence, Prohibition, and Stigma Have Paralyzed North American Responses to Opioid Overdose." *AMA Journal of Ethics* 22 (2020) 714–22. https://pubmed.ncbi.nlm.nih.gov/32880362/.

Van der Kolk, Bessel. *The Body Keeps the Score: Brain, Mind, and Body in the Healing of Trauma*. New York: Viking, 2014.

Vineyard USA. *Emotionally Focused*. Vineyard USA. https://www.emotionallyfocused.org.

Volf, Miroslav. *The End of Memory: Remembering Rightly in a Violent World*. Grand Rapids: Eerdmans, 2007.

———. *Exclusion and Embrace: A Theological Exploration of Identity, Otherness, and Reconciliation*. Nashville: Abingdon, 1996.

———. *Free of Charge: Giving and Forgiving in a Culture Stripped of Grace*. Grand Rapids: Zondervan, 2006.

Voskamp, Ann. *One Thousand Gifts: A Dare to Live Fully Right Where You Are*. Grand Rapids: Zondervan, 2010.

Welch, Edward T. *Addictions: A Banquet in the Grave: Finding Hope in the Power of the Gospel*. Phillipsburg: P & R, 2001.

Wesley, John. *The Journal of John Wesley*. 8 vols. London: Epworth, 1938.

———. *A Plain Account of Christian Perfection*. Kansas City: Beacon Hill, 1966.

Westermeyer, J. "The Role of Cultural and Social Factors in the Cause of Addictive Disorders." *Psychiatric Clinics of North America* 22 (1999) 253–73. https://pubmed.ncbi.nlm.nih.gov/10385932/.

White, William L. *Slaying the Dragon: The History of Addiction Treatment and Recovery in America*. Bloomington: Chestnut Health Systems, 2014.

Willard, Dallas. *Hearing God: Developing a Conversational Relationship with God*. Downers Grove, IL: InterVarsity, 1999.

Wine, Kenneth. "Addiction in the Workplace: Prevalence, Risks, and Strategies for Organizational Support." *Journal of Addiction Research and Therapy* 15 (2024) 722. https://www.omicsonline.org/open-access/addiction-in-the-workplace-prevalence-risks-and-strategies-for-organizational-support-134416.html.

World Health Organization. *Reducing the Harm from Alcohol by Regulating Cross-Border Alcohol Marketing, Advertising and Promotion: Executive Summary*. Geneva: WHO, May 10, 2022. https://www.who.int/publications/i/item/WHO-MSD-UCN-ADA-22-21.

———. "WHO Highlights Glaring Gaps in Regulation of Alcohol Marketing Across Borders: Young People and Heavy Drinkers Major Targets." WHO, May 10, 2022. https://www.who.int/news/item/10-15-2022-who-highlights-glaring-gaps-in-regulation-of-alcohol-marketing-across-borders.

Wright, N. T. *Paul and the Faithfulness of God*. Minneapolis: Fortress, 2013.

———. *Surprised by Hope: Rethinking Heaven, the Resurrection, and the Mission of the Church*. New York: HarperOne, 2008.

Yancey, Philip. *What's So Amazing About Grace?* Grand Rapids: Zondervan, 1997.

www.ingramcontent.com/pod-product-compliance
Lightning Source LLC
La Vergne TN
LVHW090516110826
845146LV00003B/880

* 9 7 9 8 3 8 5 2 6 2 7 3 1 *